The Temptation of the Wall

Massimo Recalcati

The Temptation
of the Wall

Five Short Lessons on Civil Life

Translated by Alice Kilgarriff

polity

Originally published in Italian as *La tentazione del muro*. Copyright © Giangiacomo Feltrinelli srl, Milano. First published in 'Varia' as *La tentazione del muro* by Massimo Recalcati, in May 2020. Published under licence of Giangiacomo Feltrinelli Editore, Milano.

This English edition © Polity Press, 2022

Polity Press
65 Bridge Street
Cambridge CB2 1UR, UK

Polity Press
101 Station Landing
Suite 300
Medford, MA 02155, USA

ISBN-13: 978-1-5095-4878-1 (hardback)
ISBN-13: 978-1-5095-4879-8 (paperback)

A catalogue record for this book is available from the British Library.
Library of Congress Control Number: 2021942282

Typeset in 12 on 15 pt Fournier MT
by Cheshire Typesetting Ltd, Cuddington, Cheshire
Printed and bound in Great Britain by CPI Group (UK) Ltd, Croydon

The publisher has used its best endeavours to ensure that the URLs for external websites referred to in this book are correct and active at the time of going to press. However, the publisher has no responsibility for the websites and can make no guarantee that a site will remain live or that the content is or will remain appropriate.

Every effort has been made to trace all copyright holders, but if any have been overlooked the publisher will be pleased to include any necessary credits in any subsequent reprint or edition.

For further information on Polity, visit our website:
politybooks.com

Contents

v

To Stefano Coletta and Pietro Galeotti, the first people to believe in this lexicon

The fateful question for the human species seems to me to be whether and to what extent their cultural development will succeed in mastering the disturbance of their communal life by the human instinct of aggression and self-destruction.

Sigmund Freud, *Civilization and Its Discontents*

Warning

This book develops the central themes of *Lessico civile*, the short television series broadcast on Italy's RAI 3 in spring 2020 and filmed prior to Christmas 2019. The collective trauma of Covid-19 had not yet reared its head. And yet, the reflections developed back then are still pertinent, even now, in the light of the tragedy that has befallen us.

Before the pandemic exploded, politics was consumed by the enormous global problem of immigration and the need to rethink how we integrate with those who are different from us. In this context, the symbol of the wall appeared as a sovereignist response to the imminent threat posed by the intruder. This sovereignism was not only a political temptation, leading to border closures, a greater military presence at those borders and the radicalization of the securitarian drive, but also reflected a profound mental inclination, as human beings have always drawn up borders, defended their own safety, rejected the risks associated with being open to the outside world.

In this context, the drive does not only manifest itself as a passion for freedom, adventure and travel, fed by a thirst for knowledge and social contact, but, as I repeatedly demonstrate in this book, it also reveals the urge to shut down, to refuse freedom, to avoid the radical responsibility this entails by choosing instead to barter it away in return for one's own security. This is the temptation to wall oneself in, which any lexicon of civility must reckon with.

The trauma of the pandemic that has swept across the entire planet since early 2020 fatally reactivates this temptation as even our friends, those closest to us, our family members could be carriers of this disease. They are all potential agents of contagion. This is the 'terroristic' nature of the virus. It separates every conventional distinction between friends and enemies, people we know and those we don't, those closest to us and those who couldn't be further away. Faceless, not really identifiable, invisible, the virus is an intruder that lives in us and among us. Its omnipresence dominates our most established defence mechanisms. Social distancing has therefore had to replicate, by force, the tightening of borders, replacing openness with sealing off, promoting division over integration.

Anxiety over contagion, coupled with the necessary defence from the rapid and violent spread of the pandemic, have brought about the imposition of extreme security measures that have objectively restricted our individual freedoms. Some people have interpreted this by evoking the spectre of the totalitarian threat of a new power founded on the biopolitical control of life. But is this really the case? Has the traumatic onslaught of Covid-19, through the unforeseen social and healthcare emergency it unleashed, paved the way for the creation of a neo-totalitarian order that poses a threat to democracy's very existence?

I do not believe so. From the perspective of freedom, the theme I have chosen to close this book of five brief lessons, the greatest lesson of this pandemic lies, in my opinion, in how it has laid bare the vacuous and purely ideological nature of freedom understood as individual property, and in how it teaches us that, ethically speaking, the greatest indicator of freedom is not that of choice or the unfurling of free will, but solidarity. Behind our being forced to give up our freedom to fight the aggression of Covid-19, there is no sacrificial phantom, no vocation for penance, nor any attack on our collective freedom, but the profound idea that no one can save themselves, that freedom without solidarity is an empty word.

When revisited in the light of this terrible emergency in which we are still fully immersed, this small book carries a message that I hope will not be ignored. It can be summed up with the words of Pier Paolo Pasolini evoking St Paul that bring this series of lessons to a close: without the word 'charity', without the word 'love', the words 'faith' and 'hope' remain shapeless and blind, in thrall to monstrous phantoms. The twentieth century saw millions of people massacred in the name of these monsters. Remembering the word 'charity' is the fundamental condition that will ensure the anonymous dimension of the multitude does not crush the irreducible character of singularity, so that we do not forget that at the basis of every lexicon of civility are the words 'welcoming', 'hospitality', 'solidarity'. Because my heart, as this little book says, is the first name of the foreigner. And so, as psychoanalysis teaches us, every process of integration starts with the friendship I extend to the foreigner I carry inside me.

Milan, 25 April 2020

Introduction

Does a lexicon of civility still exist? Are we not living in a time where our societies are marked by a new barbarianism? Have the unrestrained frenzy of the neo-libertine drive and the defence of the globalization of markets made life in the *polis* impossible? And what to say of the most recent drive for militarization at the borders and their reinforcement through the use of security forces? Where is the basic dimension of hospitality on which every human community is founded?

The neo-libertine degradation caused by hypermodern individualism and the transfiguration of the border into a wall, a stronghold, a fortress, are two sides of the same coin that define our time's lack of civility. In both cases we can identify the markers of new discontents in civilization. On the one hand is a freedom that rejects any limit (the neo-libertine drive), and on the other, we have the loss of the symbolic dimension of the border as a place of transit, and its metamorphosis into a barrier (the securitarian drive).[1]

In this book I will attempt to work through some of the fundamental junctures of our life together, using the theoretical tools provided by psychoanalysis: the figure of the foreigner, the significance of the border, of hate and of envy, the dogmatism and secularity of knowledge, fanaticism and the 'democratic mind', the anxiety brought on by freedom, the poetry of institutions and the populist mirage of their abolition. Psychoanalysis demonstrates that, in order not to collapse in on itself, mental life requires porous confines capable of feeding an exchange with alterity so as to broaden the horizon of the world. At the same time, it cannot deny the existence of a primal tendency, the drive for self-preservation, that human life uses to protect itself from the world as a place of threatening disturbances where, as Freud writes, the stranger – 'the outsider' – is met with hostility.

While freedom is a fundamental aspiration for human life, we need to recognize that it is also an object of anxiety and rejection. The psychology of the masses throughout the twentieth century has shown us the extent to which human beings have been capable of relinquishing their freedom, preferring to avoid the ethical responsibilities it implies in favour of the totalitarian chains of fascist regimes.

As we will see, truth, like freedom, is still an inalienable component of every lexicon of civility, but this does not in any way stop that same thirst for truth from sometimes tipping over into its opposite. This is the explosive blend of fanaticism: ignorance elevated to a supreme form of the truth, ignorance as the passion of one, single Truth that rejects any other possible truth.

This paradox demonstrates just how much the mental life of individuals, of groups of human beings and of institutions, is contradictory and vulnerable. Fascism is not simply a dramatic historical moment for many countries, but is a tendency that inhabits the human being. A tendency to prefer obedience to freedom, the wall to the open sea, slavery to responsibility, ignorance to knowledge, the incivility of hate to the civility of agreements and words.

In spring 2020, after presenting my *Lexicons* on love and the family, I introduced my third and final one on RAI 3: that of civility. In these written texts, developed in both their references and reasoning, the reader will find the ideas that guided the television programmes. I purposefully chose this lexicon to end the cycle.[2] Family and the loving discourse are indeed nothing if we do not consider them also in terms of the civility they are capable of generating. In the family, we have the civility of care and education, whereas in love we have that of the absolute respect for difference, for *heteros*, the only one, as Lacan explained, worthy of love.

Nevertheless, this third and final Lexicon does not take the intimate dimension of life in its singularity and its primary bonds as a starting point. Instead, it considers how this singularity has always appeared as part of the wider social dimension, which is not added to life at a later time but is a constituent part of its being. Indeed, as Homer's Telemachus declares in the opening pages of *The Odyssey*, no one has seen their own birth.[3] We are all thrown into a life that we never wanted, a life decided by the Other. Our lives are, from the outset, never without the Other. This is the idea that Freud always insisted upon: there is no individual psychology without social psychology. There is no human life that is not life immersed in a civilization.

The Border

A heart that only half beats is only half my heart. I was already
no longer inside me. I'm already coming from somewhere else, or
I'm not coming any longer at all. Something strange is disclosed
'at the heart' of the most familiar.

Jean-Luc Nancy, *The Intruder*

Roots and Freedom

Human life needs a sense of belonging, firm roots, a sense of
identity and of family. There is no lexicon of civility that does
not recognize the importance of the border. Freud constructs
psychoanalysis as a science of frontiers between the different
mental realms (the unconscious, the pre-conscious, the con-
scious) and their different internal instances (Id, Ego, Super-
Ego). Bion uses the language of psychoanalysis to emphasize
the importance of the 'contact barrier' that separates the con-
scious from the unconscious, that which is internal from the
external, the Me from the Not-Me. Without this border, life
becomes undifferentiated, indistinct, and falls into chaos.[1]

Belonging to a culture, sharing a world, filiation, genealogy,
race, descendance: the issue of identity and roots accompanies

human life from the minute it arrives in the world. There is no human life without the memory of its roots. Life comes to life without protection, steeped in despondency, exposed to the chaos of the world, submerged by its vulnerability, but the child's first scream acts as an appeal, an invocation, a cry for help from the Other. This is the fundamental sociality of existence. No one can save themselves. Without the Other, life falls into nothingness. However, in a way that might sound paradoxical, Freud imagines that the first task of life is also that of carving oneself out a protective nook in which to take refuge from the powerful and uncontrollable stimulations that come from within one's own body and from the outside world. Human life at its earliest stages resembles that of a 'bird's egg with its food supply', which must shelter that life still so defenceless and vulnerable.[2] This is the primary urge of the drive: human life must defend itself from the world, which it experiences as a source of threat. Hence the insurmountable importance of a human institution such as the family. The life of a child demands to be inscribed in a symbolic process of filiation.

We should not dismiss the human drive to defend the confines of their individual and collective lives as an urge that is inherently barbaric or uncivilized. Freud himself tells us this, pointing out how life, both individual and collective, needs protection, reassurance, that it builds barriers in order to be able to bear the adversity of the world. Human beings have always protected their own existence, whether from the inhumane might of nature or the threats of enemies. The human urge to mark their own territory is an expression of the primarily securitarian nature of this drive. The art of marking out this border is a necessary operation for our survival. Life primordially searches out refuge from life and the definition of borders that are capable of circumscribing its own identity. The uprooting that characterizes life's arrival in the world (no one chooses to be born, no one is master of their origins) is compensated for by an aspiration to become rooted in the place of the Other (be it the family, society, culture). Without roots or borders, both individual and collective subjects – the Ego and a population alike – would lack any sense of identity. It is no coincidence that, in clinical experience, it is the absence of boundaries that defines the schizophrenic life, a life that is radically lost, wandering, disintegrated, fragmented.

However, human existence is not comprised solely of a desire for belonging and reassurance, but also the urge to wander, a desire for freedom. While the desire for belonging includes individual life in a community (that of the family, for example), which offers it the right of citizenship, protection and security, that community cannot presume to encompass human life in its entirety. The desire to wander is the desire for freedom, the desire to travel, for adventure, to cross the border, and is equally important to human existence. It is no surprise, then, that the illness of an individual or a community is always somehow connected to the displacement of this relationship. While, on the one hand, an excess of belonging leads to a closing in on oneself, an erection of borders, conformism, uniformity and the exclusion of difference, on the other hand, excess wandering can lead to a severing of ties and loss of one's own identity, disorientation, bewilderment, perhaps even culminating in the loss of oneself. These are the two ways in which the splintering of the 'anthropological proportion' can occur[3] in the midst of the compelling need for the border, and the equally compelling need to move beyond it. When the sense of belonging prevails over that of freedom it creates an illness of life that, in the name of conformist adhesion to one's own culture, waives freedom, sacrificing it to the needs of that life's own security. In this case, everything that breaches the frontier, everything that lives beyond our own borders (be they individual or collective), is seen as a permanent source of threat. When, conversely, freedom and wandering overwhelm (being anthropologically disproportionate) belonging, when life is uprooted, all borders removed through the refusal of any bond or descendance, when life burns everything in the name of freedom that must be absolute, the symbolic bonds that provide us with the right to be citizens of the human community are ripped away.

The Uncivil Disease of the Wall

In his short story 'The Great Wall of China', Kafka offers a clear illustration of the pathology that can overwhelm the symbolic dimension of the border:

> Against whom was the Great Wall of China to serve as a protection? Against the people of the north. Now, I come from the south-east of China. No northern people can menace us there. We

read of them in the books of the ancients; the cruelties which they commit in accordance with their nature make us sigh beneath our peaceful trees. The faithful representations of the artist show us these faces of the damned, their gaping mouths, their jaws already furnished with great pointed teeth, their half-shut eyes that already seem to be seeking out the victim which their jaw will rend and devour. When our children are unruly we show these pictures, and at once they fly weeping into our arms. But nothing more than that do we know about these northerners. We have not seen them, and if we remain in our villages, we shall never see them, even if on their wild horses they should ride as hard as they can straight toward us – the land is too vast and would not let them reach us, they would end their course in the empty air.[4]

The stranger lives beyond the border – 'the people of the north'. As foreigners, they are an insidious threat against which we must strengthen our borders. The infinite extension of the wall, as described by Kafka, must be capable of exorcizing this threat through the creation of an unbreachable boundary. The stranger is seen as a malign and cruel entity, capable of violating the very intimacy of our own families. This is the basic principle for every one of any identity's paranoid pathological developments: every foreigner carries the risk of a nefarious contamination of our own identity. The alterity of those who live beyond the border is a danger that must be thwarted, defended against. And so, the border becomes sclerotic, shell-like, it is transformed into fences, barbed wire, walls that block everything that lies on the other side.

This pathological metamorphosis of the border forgets to consider how the symbolic function of the border is not just that of marking out our own identity (collective or individual), but also that of guaranteeing exchange, transition, communication with the stranger. This is why the great psychoanalyst Bion recognized *porosity* as one of the fundamental attributes of the border. In the rush to build up fence posts, walls, barriers, organized defences we see today, in this time seemingly dominated by an unbridled urge for security, the border risks becoming a wall that makes any exchange impossible.[5] This closure ends up prevailing over openness. That sense of belonging loses all contact with wandering and freedom. The border loses its porosity. Here, we rediscover two of the greatest forms of incivility that subvert any lexicon of civility. On the one hand is the pathology connected to the dissolution of the border, its absence, its symbolic non-inscription. This is the pathology that finds its paradigm in schizophrenia: indistinction, confusion, chaos, a lack of differentiation. It is the unilateral prevalence of uprooting over being rooted, of wandering over belonging. On the other, however, is the pathology of the border, which involves its transformation into a wall, a fortress, a stronghold. In this case, identity is paranoically hardened against any difference. The foreigner becomes a threat, a horror, the terrifying enemy we saw in Kafka's description.

Contamination Delirium

The securitarian pathology, which cedes the border to the compact and segregating figure of the wall, was the driver behind the era of totalitarianism of the twentieth century, and continues to propel all kinds of ideological fundamentalism. Its premise is a kind of *contamination delirium*, in which the foreigner is compared to a dangerous virus, a disease, an epidemic, an infection. Think of the recurring depiction of Hitler as a doctor for the Greater Germany, who would eradicate the Jewish and Communist infection from the body of the nation. We could also consider the role played more generally by Nazi medics in the regime's crazed pursuit of its preposterous ideal of collective immunization.[6] The violence of anti-Semitism and anti-Communism responds to a hygiene-driven logic of biopolitics: to purify the collective and individual body of the viruses of Communism, the Jewish, homosexuality, nomadic life and so on. The existence of the foreigner who inhabits the land beyond the border becomes a permanent threat to any purity of identity, hence the militarization of the border, incensed nationalism, racism and so on. However, this is not, as Freud pointed out, a simple barbarization of civil life. Rather, at play here is the amplification of a truly human instinct. Building up walls, fences and barriers, defending one's own house, closing, locking and bolting the doors – these are all actions that reveal the fundamental tendency of humans to search out their own protection. We are not talking about a primitive world, but the beginnings of the modern state. This is Hobbes' thesis:

'fear of death',[7] fear for one's own safety, pushes human beings to renounce freedom in exchange for protection. The wall is, therefore, a temptation that has always inhabited the human: to defend one's own life, safeguard it from any impact from the world as a source of distress and uncontrollable frenzy.

Nevertheless, a house without doors that open is no longer a house, but a fortress. This is what happens to the strange animal protagonist in Kafka's tale 'The Burrow'.[8] He is desperate to cut out the world, to build a house-burrow that excludes any possibility of encounter with or contamination by the stranger, but he never quite manages it. The rigid architectural organization of his burrow, built with meticulous care, is not able to neutralize the presence of the Other. Excluded, expelled, isolated from the burrow, the Other insists on signalling its destabilizing presence with an 'almost inaudible whistling sound' that is destined to inexorably increase in intensity to remind the burrow's mad builder that the foreigner does not come from outside but is, as Freud himself defined the unconscious, a strange, internal presence and, as such, irrepressible.[9]

No feat of engineering can exclude the existence of the Other and its strange nature. This is why Freud insists on demonstrating how, at the beginning of life, the world, a source of distress and uncontrollable frenzy, is experienced by the subject as a foreigner, and as such, *hostile*.[10] The conflation of the unknown with hostility is, again according to Freud, the result of the first instinct to overwhelm the world and, in turn, be overwhelmed by the world: the subject discovers that its protective nook is not enough to stop the levels of uncontrollable frenzy that come as much from inside its own body as from the outside.

The Temptation of the Wall

The conflation of the foreigner and hostility, the definition of the world itself as hostile due to the effect it has of upsetting the internal balance of the mental apparatus, demonstrates how the primary existence of a securitarian drive invalidates the definition of the human as a social being. If the primary characteristic of this drive is manifested as a tendency towards closing in, protection, defence of one's own individual nook, are we not then obliged to question Aristotle's well-known affirmation that humans are a 'social animal'? If, indeed, on the one hand, human life is brought into the world as a scream, an appeal, an opening towards the Other, if it carries within it the Other, because it could not exist without the Other, on the other hand, this same life manifests itself as a strenuous and anxious defence of its own boundaries, as a way of avoiding the Other, which is viewed as strange and hostile. Elias Canetti reminds us of this in *Crowds and Power*, when he evokes the shiver that runs down his spine when a stranger brushes past him in the street: 'There is nothing that man fears more than the touch of the unknown. [. . .] Man always tends to avoid physical contact with anything strange.'[11]

The unknown, the stranger, the outside and the hostile have tended to coincide from the outset. Human life is social from the outset, as it cannot exist without the support of the Other, without their word, but it is also the autistic urge towards the defence of one's own nook, one's own identity, one's own border. This is why the border is not only an atrocity or the result of political illiteracy, but a real passion for humans, their fundamental temptation.

Donald Trump won the 2016 US presidential elections through a shameless endorsement of this passion. In his most famous speeches, the wall is presented as fundamental to the nation's identity, as a necessary defence against the Mexican danger. But it would be wrong, and naïve, to think that the hostile existence of the Mexicans is what actually creates the need for a wall. As we see with the strange animal in Kafka's tale, the danger we really need to defend ourselves against is the very existence of the stranger. It is therefore the need for the wall that is primary, rather than the presence of the Mexicans, who simply provide its political justification.

The First Face of the Foreigner

The foreigner is not only the person who lives on the other side of the border, the strange, ferocious and evil people whom Kafka described in his short story on the Chinese wall. Children depict the foreigner as a dangerous animal, a werewolf, an ogre, a monster, a bogeyman, a wild dog, an alien. The stranger is the threatening figure who breaks into their bedrooms and haunts their dreams. Children with no concept of prejudice (except that gained from their parents) nevertheless experience this fear of the bogeyman, an unknown monster or, as happens to little

Hans in Freud's *Analysis of a Phobia*, horses and other animals viewed as dangerous. In fact, childhood animal phobias are the first form of defence against the disturbing nature of life, as embodied by the animal. But they are also a form of defence against the risk of madness.

The human being fears their own madness just as the child fears the animal's indomitable nature. Madness and the animal are able to externally embody our inability to control our own internal instincts. Think of the legendary *Ship of Fools* as depicted by Bosch, which drags the mad into the water, pulling them away from dry land where their city is under siege. The overflowing of madness causes anxiety for human beings, who have always carried that madness within them. As Foucault astutely points out, the mad in the modern age have taken the position previously occupied by lepers in the Middle Ages.[12] Madness, like leprosy, represents an uncontainable and ever-present threat. Hence the acts of expulsion and segregation, in which we find once more the human temptation to separate normality from abnormality, reason from a lack of reason, impurity from the pure, infection from the healthy.

But just as Freud, and later Basaglia in his interpretation of Freud, tried to demonstrate, madness is not the anti-human, but the very essence of being human. Indeed, the rigid confine between normality and madness only responds to a protective finality: moving away, excluding and segregating the alterity of the stranger, of the monster we carry within us. The crucial importance of Basaglia's work is that of considering madness, against any phobic-expulsive temptation, to be an expression of the human condition and not a regression to an animal-like state. All of his work against mental institutions was based on the idea of demonstrating how madness has every right to full citizenship in the human *polis*, that it is not a malevolent deviation from the human but its radical expression.[13] In this case also, we once again have to avoid strengthening the border separating normality from madness. Madness cannot be resolved through its expulsion or reclusion, through its being uprooted from the terra firma of reason, or through its being segregated away, because, as Lacan would say, it remains a manifestation of humans' radical and dramatic freedom.[14]

The Fearful Sensation of Life

One of psychoanalysis' greatest discoveries is that mental illness does not come from the collapse of the border that separates reason and non-reason, but rather, it is a result of this border being excessively rigid. Madness is not caused by an excessive fragility of the Ego, but by its hypertrophic reinforcement. The wild animal or bogeyman that scare children at night are a manifestation of the anarchic nature of drive. This is why the first name of the stranger paradoxically coincides with our own lives. Those first erections cause little Hans anxiety because he experiences not having any control over his own body. The body of drives eludes any intentional control by the conscience. The stranger, before being the foreigner who lives beyond the border, is that which runs through my entire existence: they are the internal stranger, the unconscious as 'internal unknown territory'. This is what Lacan means when he refers to the 'sensation of life' and our own body as a chosen site of anxiety:

> What are we afraid of? Of our body. This is what the curious phenomenon [. . .] which I called anxiety shows. In our body, precisely, anxiety is situated somewhere other than fear. It is the feeling that arises from the presentiment that comes to reduce us to our bodies.[15]

Is it truly possible to think that our own living body can provoke fear? Take the heart. No one can control its beating. Its beating is like an intruder, a foreigner that is, however, inside me, that is me. An alterity that is one with my very existence, an 'internal stranger'. Could our heart be the real first face of the stranger? A panic attack proves the uncontrollable nature of this internal presence (the heartbeat) on which my life depends completely, but over which it has no dominion. Listening to one's own heartbeat can, as we see with panic attacks, become an anxiety-provoking and alienating experience.

This is what happened to one of my patients who, as they were falling asleep, had their first panic attack because they were paying close attention to their heartbeat. Whilst proving itself to be entirely autonomous, their heartbeat grew fatally irregular under the stress of excessive vigilance. The subject was panicked because they experienced their own heart as an internal foreign presence.

The Intruder

An autobiographical tale by the philosopher Jean-Luc Nancy powerfully highlights the significance of the border as a definition of identity and a porous location of exchange. However, it also demonstrates the risk of its potential sclerosis. In a piece he wrote for a special edition of a philosophy journal dedicated to the theme of 'The Foreigner's Arrival', Nancy unexpectedly decided to discuss his recent heart transplant, made necessary due to serious cardiac disease. In order for the philosopher's life to continue, it was necessary for another's heart to be implanted into his own body. Without this transplant, his life would have ended. The intrusion here reveals another face characterizing life's first impact from the world. The urge for security refuses the distress of the foreign and hostile world as an upsetting intrusion. However, in the case of Nancy's personal experience, the heart of a stranger, and its intrusion, are necessary in order for life to continue. Intrusion here is not a trauma that generates anxiety, but the opening up of a possibility for life to reclaim life.

I need to add one more element to complete this refined and dramatic metaphor of civil life: the clinical condition that makes an organ transplant work is the lowering of the immune defences. If the defence is too strong, the new heart (the heart of the stranger, the Jewish person, the traveller, the homosexual, the black man, the Polish woman) will be rejected. This is referred to in clinical settings as 'rejection crisis'. The border must be porous in order to allow both the transplant and the body's acceptance of the new heart. At the same time, however, the weakening of the immune system fatally leads to the unleashing of viruses and other pathologies from within the body, which had until that point existed only in a nebulous state of dormancy. An invisible parade of internal foreign presences awakens, strangers of all kinds arise from the remote oblivion of internal organs. They do not come from beyond the border, but from within the confines of the body itself:

> Identity is equal to immunity, the one is identified with the other. To lower the one is to lower the other. Strangeness and being a stranger become common, everyday things. This gets translated through a constant exteriorization of myself: I have to be measured, checked, tested. We are flooded with warnings about the outside world (crowds, stores, swimming pools, little children, sick people). But our liveliest enemies are within: old viruses crouching all along in the shadows of immunity, having always been there, intruders for all time.[16]

The experience of the heart transplant, in the way Nancy tells it, appears as an intense metaphor for democracy. The fall of the border brings about the collapse of a life invaded by viruses of all kinds. But the strengthening of this same border stops life from restarting. In order for life to stay alive, it must contend with the (sometimes dramatic) difficulty inherent in the process of inclusion and integration. If the border stops being a place of transit, turning instead into a rigid wall, life dies, it is starved of oxygen, the heart stops beating. If the immune defence is too strong, the heart transplant fails and life dies. In order for there to be life, it is necessary to keep the border porous without turning it into a wall. We must play host to the heart of another in order to live. The greatest danger, as we have pointed out, is that of expulsion, of rejection crisis. It is necessary to weaken the function of the immune system, to reactivate transit with the Other. This is the only way the stranger's heart can take the place of our own and bring us back to life. Is this not the great lesson taught by civility and democracy?

Particularly striking is an extraordinary American story. Bill Conner is a father who lost his twenty-year-old daughter in 2017. He decided to bike through the United States, cycling for four thousand kilometres from Wisconsin to Florida, to meet the young man who had received his daughter's heart and ask if he could listen to that heart beating once more, using a stethoscope. The heart is his daughter's, but it now beats inside a different body. This is a poetic and extremely human example of inclusion as the first definition of any lexicon of civility.

We Are All Foreigners

The border defines an identity and cannot avoid the question of hospitality. While hospitality without identity leads to chaos, identity without hospitality is death. Homer's *Odyssey* recounts Ulysses' vicissitudes as he encounters foreign lands and people. During his tortuous return journey, the king of Ithaca meets different peoples, visits lands that are enchanted, unknown, he encounters gods, humans who speak different languages, he crosses all the borders of the world, even the forbidden border imposed by Hades that separates life and death. His actions are, as we know, informed by his innate *hybris*.

But Ulysses himself is a foreigner, a migrant, defeated and without a homeland. He is not only the king of Ithaca or the brave leader in the Trojan War, but the symbol of shipwreck. His is a life lost at sea, abandoned to its own fate. Nausicaa, the young princess from the kingdom of Phaeacia, is the symbol of a border, a foreign land (the island of Phaeacia), that does not deny hospitality to the 'poor shipwrecked' Ulysses, but takes care of him:

> Stand, my maidens. Whither do ye flee at the sight of a man? Ye do not think, surely, that he is an enemy? That mortal man lives not, nor exists nor shall ever be born who shall come to the land of the Phaeacians as a foeman [. . .] Nay, this is some hapless wanderer that has come hither. Him must we now tend; for from Zeus are all strangers and beggars, and a gift, though small, is welcome. Come, then, my maidens, give to the stranger food and drink, and bathe him in the river in a spot where there is shelter from the wind.[17]

In this scene, Ulysses is like the foreign heart that lives inside each of us. It is to this heart – this symbol of the alterity inherent in the Other – that we must show hospitality so that life may stay alive. The stranger is not the enemy. This is what the princess Nausicaa shows us when faced with this nameless castaway. This is the ethical foundation of any lexicon of civility: the recognition of the Law of the word, of the order of language as our shared foreign land.

2

Hate

Hate is a career without limit.

Jacques Lacan, *Freud's Papers on Technique 1953–1954*[1]

The Passion of Hate

Hate is not the same as simple aggression. Its aim is not a competitive attack on an enemy or adversary. Hate does not come from an impulsive response, it is not generated in the chaos of a fight, physical or otherwise. Unlike aggression, hate has the status of a real passion that focuses anxiety, substituting it with the object of hate, as happens in other ways with phobias.

Indeed, in childhood phobias, anxiety is overcome through the placement of fear onto one single object. Little Hans' fear of horses temporarily solves the problem of his anxiety, as it becomes enough to avoid that object (in this case, horses) in order to avoid any confrontation with the uncontrollable nature of his own body of drives.

Something similar happens with hate. Rather than facing up to one's own anxiety – the anxiety of one's own body of drives, one's own malevolence, one's own impurity – it is preferable to pinpoint an (impure) object onto which all hate is unloaded.

Unlike what happens with phobias, there is no *avoidance of the object*, but *rage against it*. In this way, hate gives a face and an identity to the evil that actually lives in the subject itself, and which the subject is incapable of recognizing. This is why the passion of hate offers a certain level of solidity. The tremor of anxiety does not exist, instead there is this force that identifies the danger causing the subject's unhappiness, their deep unease, their malevolence, as an external object.

While aggression is therefore a temporary response destined to dissolve within a short time, to be consumed in the impetus of the impulsive reaction when faced with the imagined rival, hate is a stable consolidation of aggression, a passion focused on destroying, cancelling out, dragging down and slandering the human dignity of the object of that hate. Its practice is not angry, dissociated or haphazard, but enacted with determination in the name of the subject's purity against the contaminated, the degenerate, the impure.

This is what we see very clearly in Nazi hate towards the Jewish people. The violence of hate implies the dehumanization of the hated subject, their malign representation as rapacious, unworthy, subhuman. The ferocious hate of the pure is always justified by the unworthy nature of the impure. For this reason, the condition of the hated subject does not depend on what they say or do, but what they are. It is a hate for their existence because it is different from mine. Pure hate is always, in this sense, ontologically racist. Its fundamental barbarism is this: *transforming the Other's diversity into a moral deformity*.

Hate is the treatment of one's own evil through its protective projection onto the 'evil' object. This is the sadistic component that usually accompanies hate. Sadism is, in fact, an apathetic, lucid passion, like that of the torturer who not only wants to extort a confession from their victim, but wants also to annihilate their freedom, their alterity, destroying their dignity and mortifying their existence.

Hate is Older than Love

Freud says that hate is older than love, and that it expresses the refusal of the foreign world by the mental apparatus as a source of uncontrollable and disturbing stimulations.[2] Hate is older than love because, as we have just seen, it expresses life's urge to defend itself from its own life. Freud believed its pathematic basis could be found in *spitting*: expelling that which makes us suffer, keeping that which hurts us far from ourselves. This has an added problem, however, that results in an undeniable reality: *you cannot spit out drive*. Hate would like to externally dispose of that which inhabits the subject, its own body of drives.

Its endeavour is primarily defensive: the difficulty of symbolizing the stranger inside incites hate towards the stranger outside. This is this first form of hate, the most archaic: to expel what cannot be controlled, to separate the good (inside) from the bad (outside), the pleasure of displeasure, spitting out the evil that lives inside me.

In the analytical lexicon, the mental evolution of the act of spitting defines the category of *projection*. It is an unconscious process by which what is impossible to recognize inside is transferred outside. I can give some very simple examples: the dogged censor that is actually disproportionately attracted to everything they censor; the homophobe nurturing an unconscious homosexuality they are in no way willing to recognize. In both cases, the part of the body of drives that the subject cannot accept, cannot make compatible with their own Ego, is split, projected, externalized and unloaded through hate.

Hate or the Word?

The violence that feeds the clash of political and social forces can erupt from frustration, poverty and injustice. Conflict can be unleashed when the symbolic dialectic between parts of society or different generations is interrupted. But when hate is unleashed by desperation, it is not comparable to the lucid passion we have just described. Rather, it is generated through the absence of a response by the Other (state, society, institutions).

The violent revolts of the most marginalized classes and the hate towards representatives of the state can, in these cases, be explained by the misery of the rebels' living conditions and their sense of having been abandoned by politics. Social hate can flourish when no one listens to the desperation with which the most fragile and socially vulnerable classes make their demands, when their request is unheeded, ignored, denied. The degeneration of political conflict into violence can be caused by desperation, which is a radical form of freedom: the freedom of those who react to the absence of freedom, the freedom of those who resist the destruction of their own freedom. Desperation is an extreme form of the resistance of freedom when this is attacked and overwhelmed by power. It flows from the misery of absolute abandonment and is, at the same time, an expression of the refusal to be abandoned into the void of the death drive.

In any case, the violence unleashed by hate interrupts the symbolic regime of the word. It is a fact of individual and collective experience. As long as there is dialogue, as long as the word is being used, there is no violence. When there is violence, the word is interrupted, its Law is questioned. This Law excludes the violent act as a matter of principle, except when the violence of hate also takes control of language. In this case, the language of violence stops any communication, turning it into insult, injury, defamation. The word is distorted, it loses all symbolic value and assimilates with the rock, the fist, the bullet.

This happens, for instance, with slander, when actions or thoughts are attributed to someone who has never carried them out, with the sole aim of discrediting them. The meaning of words, then, no longer has any value, only how and to what extent they can be used to attack. This is why there is almost never a real debate in political conflict, only a caricature of the adversary, with everyone moulding their adversary to the caricatured-instrumentalized representation that best suits them when trying to make their point.

The violence of hate is not only manifested in the caricatured distortion of the word, but can also lead to the word's cancellation, to its suppression, to its misrecognition. It undermines the right of the word on which every lexicon of civility is based.

If conflict, when it assumes political dignity, contributes to the symbolic channelling of violence, the passage to violent action without conflict is unleashed by the de-structuring of the political sphere. Here, there is no political conflict, only violence, hate, an urge to destroy and make the enemy inhumane. Violence without democratic political conflict is blind. Conversely, political conflict within the realm of democracy tends to be a way of sublimating the obtusely mindless dimension of violence.

There are, however, moments when conflict is regressively brought back to blind violence. This happens when the political is obscured by the ontological. For example, with racial discrimination, it is the fundamental barbarism of hate that wants to degrade its enemy beyond the Law of language, beyond Law, beyond the city. The basis for every lexicon of civility is, as we have seen, our belonging as human beings to the homeland of language, and it is precisely this foundation that hate aims to destroy. While the word achieves its aims through tortuous paths and articulated passages, through the effort and patience of dialogue, the violence of hate prefers to hit its target in just one strike, eliminating anyone who gets in its way. It aims to replace the tortuousness inherent in the mediation of the word and of politics with the arrogance of those who simply want to eliminate their own adversary.

Hate as an Alternative to the Painful Labour of Mourning

For psychoanalysis, hate is without thought or mind. It takes the place of a mourning that has never been carried out. It is the result of an impossible labour of mourning. We must not forget that thought itself comes from mourning. A child begins to think when they have been exposed to the loss of the breast. The same goes for the word. A child can only talk because they have lost the breast, they have experienced its irreversible absence. Their mouth is empty, without object, and is therefore available not just to suction, but to the word.

Conversely, hate flows from an intolerance when faced with mourning, with the tragic and irreversible experience of the loss. In this sense it is similar to a hallucination. The loss does not call for the long labour of thought, but the short circuit of a hallucination that aims to magically heal the wound. We see this in a case described by Freud. A young mother loses her long-awaited new-born child. But rather than mourning and processing this extremely painful loss, she walks the hospital corridors with a piece of wood wrapped in blankets, calling it by the dead child's name.[3]

To be even clearer, let's take the example of a loving separation. It is not unusual for a violent act, driven by blind hate for those who have abandoned us, to be the response to the insurmountable difficulty of processing the loss of the loved object.

This happens in a dramatic way with femicide. Rather than processing the narcissistic wound caused by separation, some men resort to the madness of violence. Rather than mourning the painful death of a love, they brutally sentence to death the person who has left them, designating themselves as avengers.

The psychoanalytical and anthropological reflections of Franco Fornari on the phenomenon of war confirm the thesis of hate as a way of avoiding the painful labour of mourning. In this sense, war itself is the result of a paranoid refusal of the symbolic process of mourning.[4]

For some communities in Sub-Saharan Africa, for example, rather than triggering a time of mourning, the death of a child can lead to a declaration of war with the neighbouring community, driven by the idea that their shaman has been responsible for the death of that child. This is an example of the protective-paranoid function of the human mind that, in order to avoid the pain of mourning, attributes the cause of the loss to the evil of a stranger. This is a primary tendency of the drive: to unload our own difficulty in thinking about what hurts us most onto the hated object.

Envious Hate

There is, however, a more subtle form of hate on which psychoanalysis in particular has focused its attentions: that of the envious hate that affects who we would like to be and are not. It is the hate that attacks not the stranger – the deformed object that lives beyond the border – but those closest to us, those who embody the ideal that 'I' would like to be and cannot. We have its mythical incarnation in the biblical episode where Cain kills his brother Abel. According to Lacan, in order to truly understand this scene, we must consider another mythological figure, who does not belong to the biblical world but that of the classics: Narcissus.[5] Indeed, Narcissus and his suicidal dream of adhering perfectly to his own ideal image is the true, inescapable reference required to fully understand Cain's bloody act. Cain strikes his brother because Abel embodies his own narcissistic, and unobtainable, ideal. God shows that he prefers Abel's gifts to those proffered by Cain, he shows he loves one more than the other:

> CAIN: I just wanted a little love, I just wanted my offering to be accepted. A sign, even a modest one that said, that's fine, that's just fine. What you do is good, all the fruits of your labour are good. My struggles are immense.[6]

Cain's feelings of envy, which will lead him to end his brother's life, stem from the privilege God affords Abel.

In order to understand this human urge to envious destruction, therefore, we must consider not just the social dimension of frustration, but the narcissistic dimension of fascination. There is a profoundly suicidal and self-destructive component to envious hate. Narcissus loses his life whilst attempting in vain to achieve his ideal image as reflected in the water, as the painting of Narcissus attributed to Caravaggio admirably demonstrates. The same thing happens to Cain when he is faced with Abel.

The drama of envious hate always takes place before a mirror. I observe with sadness and hate the full life of the person I envy, access to which is impossible for me. Envy always implies a relationship with an ideal Other who is hated because they are incomparable. The one who is envied is always what the envious person would like to be, consciously or otherwise, but is unable to achieve. The object of envy is never someone who is marginalized, secondary, insignificant. This is the thesis put forward by Melanie Klein: it is not the breast without nutrition that gives rise to envy, but the one overflowing with life, the most generous breast. For this reason, we only bite the hand that feeds us.[7]

The envious person never envies just something, such as a possession or quality of the individual, but their very life. The envious person is poor of life and envies the rich life that overflows with life. The desperation shown by Caligula, the bloodthirsty emperor who was depicted by Camus, demonstrates clearly how at the centre of envious hate there is, in reality, an unextinguishable void, a poverty of life. The envious life can spread only death. The great emperor sees his life like that of a dried-out tree trunk. With his hate and hunger for power he tries, in vain, to compensate for an unquenchable 'great void'.

I shan't have the moon. But how bitter it is to be right, and to have to go on until the consummation! Because I am scared of the consummation. Listen! The sound of arms. It is innocence preparing for victory. Why am I not there? I am scared. How disgusting, after having despised others, to feel the same cowardice within my soul. But it doesn't matter. Fear doesn't last either. The great void in which the heart is soothed will return.[8]

Envy of Life

Envious sentiment erodes the social bond, it nullifies any sense of gratitude, it cancels out memory. Cain forgets his brotherly bond with Abel, the Kleinian child forgets how much it owes to the breast that has fed it, Judas forgets how much he has savoured the words of his Master.[9] The real object of envy is never something that belongs to the individual, or one of their characteristics. What the envious person envies to the point of death is the vital force of the one they envy, their superior ability to be alive, their most alive of lives. Fundamentally, as Lacan pointed out, envious hate is pure *Lebensneid*, envy of life.[10]

There are two particularly emblematic examples we can consider. The first is from the film *Amadeus* (1984), by Miloš Forman, which focuses on Salieri's envy of the young and impetuously talented Mozart. It is clear that Salieri's envy of his genius rival is not just envy of the talent to which Salieri is privy, but above all envy of Mozart's life, his most alive life, his generative force, his smile.

The second example is far more disturbing but dramatically in keeping with the first. It is the case of a murder that occurred on 23 February 2019 at the Murazzi in Turin. A murder committed because the young assassin couldn't bear the presence of a smile on his victim's face. The same smile as that of young Mozart, which Salieri found unbearable. His murderous gesture had no defined motive other than an inability to tolerate that smile as a sign of a life more alive than his own.

That young man's smile seemed sarcastic, while the life of his murderer was without smiles, excluded from the splendour of life, a life without light, without hope. The statement he gave the police after murdering Stefano Leo and immediately handing himself in leaves us lost for words: there was no motive except the happiness of a stranger. It is because of this happiness that his hand took up a knife and slit his victim's throat in this most abominable, sacrificial rite. 'I picked him because it seemed like he had a happy life.' These few words were the only ones he could find with which to explain his crazed actions.

Perhaps in this way he would have been able to get a little of the media spotlight? There was, indeed, no relationship, no tension, no animosity, no unfinished business between the killer and his victim. No crazed voice that had ordered the act. Just two young men, strangers, one of whom decides to take the other's life for the simple reason that he seemed to have a happier one. Were these two men placed before a tragically jeering mirror? The killer's life had gone off the rails, and was in a moment of crisis he believed could never be fixed: separated from his wife, forbidden from seeing his children, unemployed, lonely. The victim's life was entirely unknown, its only crime was smiling, seeming happier than others. This is the scene of the crime. Jealous envy its only motive.

Whilst the drive behind the lucid passion of hate responds to the friend–enemy conflict, to antagonism between differences, between radical and irreducible differences, envy always implies a close proximity between the envious and the envied. Aristotle said we don't feel envy towards those who do not belong to our world, only to those who are like us, not too different from us, only the luckiest, the richest, the most alive. While hate lends itself to being utilized by politics, arming the hand against strangers, against antagonists, against those who are different, envy is more devious, encouraging resentment against those who are like me but (undeservedly) have more than me. Envy is always blind because it is aimed at those who are like us and have more than us, in an attempt to discredit them. This is why defamation is the most expressive form of envy.

But if we were to push right to the crux of our analysis of envy, the only object of envy we would find would be life itself. One obviously cannot feel envious of a life that is lived in misery, depressed, a life that is extinguished. Envy is always envy for a full life. The innocent guilt of the young man murdered in the crowd was to have smiled, to have more light in his face than others. The same as Mozart under Salieri's bitter gaze. The desperation of the envious cannot bear the richness of other's people's lives. It is no coincidence that, for the Catholic Church, the vice of envy is closely linked to that of arrogance, to love of one's own excellence (*amor propriæ excellentiæ*), which cannot tolerate the envied subject's success. Etymologically speaking, envy comes from the Latin *invidere*, which means 'not able to see', 'to not bear being seen', 'to look at with hatred'. Dante refers to it as a gaze that cannot see well, closed within the dense half-light of Purgatory. The eyes of the envious are perforated and sewn together with iron thread. They lean on one another, herded together in a shapeless, lacerated mass.[11]

We live in a time that constantly feeds envy instead of struggle and conflict against injustice. It has outclassed social critique and the justified demands of the weakest, at times even penetrating the dynamics of politics itself with disastrous consequences: privatizing conflict, making it endless, promoting destruction as an end in itself instead of the fight for emancipation. On social media, as on our streets, those who still know how to smile risk becoming the target of the envy of others who feel excluded by the richness of life. This is the sad gaze of the envious, corrupted by the joy of others, without a future. For Thomas Aquinas, envy is the only one of the seven deadly sins that does not involve any active enjoyment. These is no enjoyment, no benefit, no pleasure other than the torment caused by the joy of others, and 'chagrin at the good of another'.[12]

3

Ignorance

When the growing individual finds that he is destined to remain
a child for ever, that he can never do without protection against
strange superior powers, he lends those powers the features
belonging to the figure of his father; he creates for himself the
gods whom he dreads, whom he seeks to propitiate, and whom he
nevertheless entrusts with his own protection.

Sigmund Freud, *The Future of an Illusion*

The Father-as-Master

The patriarchal family is dominated by the severe and judgemen-
tal word of the father-as-master. His aura is one of silence mixed
with fear and uneasy respect. The patriarchal father's authority
effectively extinguishes all discourse, making the unique practice of the word impossible. This is why Freud theorized that in
mass psychology, the inflexible and hypnotic gaze of the leader
preproduces that of the 'primal father'.[1] His children, like the
masses, are subjected to the unbridled power of the boss.

In this sense, the patriarchal figure of the father contradicts
the symbolic function of the father. This function should actually be one that, first and foremost, is capable of providing

the word and guaranteeing its plural circulation. The father in psychoanalysis is not the virile man with a beard and moustache, as in the stereotypical depiction favoured by patriarchal ideology, he is not one and the same as the real father. He is not simply the parent of his children, but the very symbol of the Law of the word and its role of humanizing life, whilst ensuring the ignition and transmission of desire. He is the symbol of the word capable of humanizing the word, who does not have to be the real father, or the child's creator, but can manifest himself anywhere and through anything.[2]

However, when it comes to the repressively sterile word of the father-as-master, the Law falls on life with the force of an axe, a whip, a punishment that knows no forgiveness. With the added effect of burdening the children with guilt for the anxiety their transgressive behaviour might cause for their parents, as is powerfully demonstrated in Michael Haneke's 2009 film *The White Ribbon*. It is the rebellious life of these children that makes the father's severe punishment necessary, as he must bring this life into step with the moralistic ideals of an upright life. Indeed, all authoritarian education aims to regulate the life of our children, subjecting them to a kind of disciplinary dressage. This kind of education ignores the existence of the child's secret, of their desire as different, divergent, orphaned and necessarily heretical.[3] All authoritarian education would like to transform the irregularity of every child into a life passively adapted to the culture of the head of the family.

This is one of the most uncivilized and dangerous manifestations of ignorance. The disciplinary exercise of power demands a sacrificial submission to the Law of the father-as-master. It suppresses the right to the word and to criticism, it views dangerous diversions from this as heresies that must be reabsorbed and brought back to the right path. All authoritarian institutions seem to correspond to the family in *The White Ribbon*. This is, as we have seen, Freud's thesis: the infatuated gaze of the authoritarian leader reflects the hypnotic power of the patriarchal father. Children, like the masses, have no right to freedom, just the duty of obedience and submission.

The Consolidation of Ignorance

We might define the tendency of human life to fabricate a dogmatic version of the truth that demands a relationship of fideistic adoration as 'fundamentalism'. In this sense, fundamentalism can be political, religious or cultural. Its common denominator is that one Truth imposes ignorance of other possible truths. The essence of every fundamentalism is to consolidate ignorance, to posit (more precisely) *ignorance as the foundation of an absolute truth*.

In this way, ignorance is no longer a defect, a lack of knowledge, but, just like hate, it becomes a bona fide passion. The passion of ignorance coincides with its demand to be the master of truth. We can find a very good example in 'prejudice', which is nothing but a consolidated ignorance that aims to present itself as the unequivocal manifestation of the truth. The most profound trait of all fundamentalism consists in exercising ignorance, starting with the idea of possessing the truth in an exclusive way. This is its explosive blend: *mixing ignorance with truth*.

The passion of ignorance is at the heart of the recent auto-biographical novel *Educated*, written by Tara Westover. Her Mormon family's religious fanaticism forbids any understanding of God other than a severe and sadistic presence who threatens the imminent end of the world – the 'Days of Abomination':

> I am only seven, but I understand that it is this fact, more than any other, that makes my family different: we don't go to school.
>
> Dad worries that the Government will force us to go but it can't, because it doesn't know about us. Four of my parents' seven children don't have birth certificates. We have no medical records because we were born at home and have never seen a doctor or nurse. We have no school records because we've never set foot in a classroom. When I am nine, I will be issued a Delayed Certificate of Birth, but at this moment, according to the state of Idaho and the federal government, I do not exist.
>
> Of course I *did* exist. I had grown up preparing for the Days of Abomination, watching for the sun to darken, for the moon to drip as if with blood. I spent my summers bottling peaches and my winters rotating supplies. When the World of Men failed, my family would continue on, unaffected.[4]

Growing up in Idaho, in a far-flung valley surrounded by tall mountains and thick forest, Tara was educated according to the strictest Mormon teachings: no medicines, no vaccines, no books, no television, no friends, no driving licence, no telephone, no birth certificate ('I knew I'd been born near the end of September, and each year I picked a day'),[5] but most importantly, absolutely no school.

Dominating it all is the figure of a father, depicted with heart-wrenching tragic force, a father from another time who believes in carrying out the will of a furious and vengeful God on earth. This is a terrifying version of the father-as-master, upheld by patriarchal ideology. This man's religious delirium is at the centre of his family's life. Always busy building refuges, like a crazed Noah, accumulating and boxing up supplies, rifles and petrol, sacks of grain and kegs of honey so that his family may survive the 'Days of Abomination', the final catastrophe that will destroy the evildoers who inhabit the earth and save the pure, this man embodies a wild and obsessive authority, a crazed version of the Law. According to his religious delirium, 'socialists', 'infidels', 'Illuminati spies' populate the outside world, posing a constant threat. It is therefore necessary for the family to barricade themselves inside their house, like the Kafkian character in 'The Burrow', in a fortress without windows or doors. While the family – the burrow – is Good, the world is Evil.

But Tara's tragic discovery, which ends up freeing her from this prison, is that the devil is not outside, but in there with them. That the horrors are not out there in the world, but belong to this non-existent God and his terrestrial spokesman who throws around curses and predicts disasters. The discovery that had the most decisive impact on her future was that Evil was inside her family and not outside it, as her father's teachings would have it.

Her brother Shawn – most likely a dangerous paranoiac – visits all kinds of violence upon her: he twists her arms, suffocates her, forces her head under water, crushes her against the pavement, insults her ('Whore!'), pulls her by her hair, threatens her with a knife and – when she is finally on the other side of the world, far from her family – wounds her with emails that are like bullets fired from afar with murderous intent.

The world of men in that family seems to be polarized around these two extremes, which only appear as opposites, given that the paternal devotion to the Law of God and the brutal use of violence by the brother are, in reality, two sides of the same coin. Indeed, when no space is left for *heteros*, when there is no respect for alterity, life becomes hell, and the Law the place of a chaotic and disruptive will.

Her mother, a herbalist and midwife, 'said she could feel the hot energy moving through our bodies'.[6] Her ability with homeopathic medicine is the result of an intimate exchange with God. Through her hand and her eyes, it is God who takes care of those poor souls to whom this woman dedicates herself with a profound sense of duty. Her position in terms of her husband is one of defenceless obedience. The same goes for the violence continually unleashed by her paranoid son on his sisters. She puts up no defence, offering nothing but tragically silent consent.

Tara seems destined for a life of collecting, carving up and welding scrap metal, working in the junkyard alongside her father and brothers with her steel-capped boots, living submerged in a closed world that views the outside world as a perpetual threat.

But, as Freud believed, life is not the passive prey of its childhood. Tara Westover's story demonstrates how, while the traumatic traces of one's past may continuously afflict one's body and soul, the child's life always has the possibility of giving a new form to its own story. This is why the child striving for poetry needs new oxygen to flourish. This happens for Tara, as it does for many children, through her encounter with School. First college, and then university, are unforeseen deviations from her predestined life. Changes of direction, changes of pace that make a new poem possible. A long and tragic apprenticeship is required in order to learn a language different from the (fundamentalist) language of her family. Thanks to School, Tara is finally able to introduce herself to the unknown and fascinating plurality of other languages. Whilst her father believed School to be an illness that kept children dangerously far from God, for Tara it becomes the location of an extraordinary opening towards new knowledge, the opportunity for a vital new departure. Faced with the crossroads that separates her from her roots, Tara doesn't hesitate, instead powerfully assuming her own desire for knowledge, another thing that was held hostage by her family in every possible way:

> What is a person to do, I asked, when their obligations to their family conflict with *other* obligations – to friends, to society, to themselves? [. . .] You could call this selfhood many things. Transformation. Metamorphosis. Falsity. Betrayal. I call it an education.[7]

However, no education can take place by cancelling the past. The process of subjectivization and separation always implies a jump forward from what has already gone before. For this reason, at the end of her tortuous journey, Tara can, for example, recognize that it was the hours spent at the desk deciphering the 'narrow strands of Mormon doctrine' that helped her develop the 'patience to read things I could not yet understand':

> In retrospect, I see that *this* was my education, the one that would matter: the hours I spent sitting at a borrowed desk, struggling to parse narrow strands of Mormon doctrine in mimicry of a brother who'd deserted me. The skill I was learning was a crucial one, the patience to read things I could not yet understand.[8]

Any child striving for poetry is always working with remnants, the ashen remains of the language of fathers. The road to liberation from the ignorance of the single language of one's own family always implies a tear, a narrow passage, a rupture. But every existence nevertheless carries with it the traces of its own past, it is marked by those traces that, however, are able to find another form of scripture. For this reason, our past never lies motionless behind us, but re-signifies itself, acquires new meaning but only as we move towards the future.

The Democracy of Books

As we have seen, all dogmatic fundamentalism maintains absolute truths that clash with a secular concept of knowledge. Tara

Westover's delirious father is emblematic of this. It was no coincidence that Freud saw psychoanalysis as secular by definition (*Laienanalyse*).

The etymology of the German word *laien* reveals precisely this meaning: to ignore the basic truths, absolute, incontrovertible truths. The truths of fundamentalism function like prejudice, because they impose themselves as incontrovertible truths, and thus as extreme forms of ignorance. They are truths that come before thought, before critical judgement, which are, by definition, prejudicial. This is why the free spirit is the antagonist of every dogmatic version of truth.

An epic description of the barbarism of fundamentalism is the biblical myth of the people of Babel. They are obsessed by the idea of building 'a single people', 'a single language', of 'making a name for themselves'.[9] They are a people who 'challenge God' in the name of their own omnipotence. If God is the location of the Law of the word that must conserve the pluralism of all languages, the Babylonians believe it necessary to challenge the power of God in order to impose their own single language, their own absolute truth. Challenging God, as the fundamentalism of the people of Babel does, means wanting to destroy the plurality of languages, which is at the basis of any lexicon of civility and the democratic life of the *polis*. Monolingualism makes any experience of democracy impossible. For this reason, the biblical God intervenes with the Babylonians, demolishing the illusion of a single language, dispersing, stratifying and multiplying the languages, forcing humans to translate in order to understand one another. As we see in Walter Benjamin's wonderful definition, democracy is the need for translation. No population is the master of language, no single language can be imposed on the multiplicity of other languages.

If fundamentalism consists in the reduction of the multiplicity of languages to one single language, if its basis is the consolidation of the ignorance of other languages, then democracy has the task of preserving that multiplicity of languages. It is no surprise that books are hated and burned by all dictatorships. All forms of fascism have always used censorship, they have thrown books into the fire along with the divergent ideas contained within them. Books do not exist, only the Book: the Book of Books. The Book which, by feeding the ignorance of other books, arms us against books. Indeed, the existence of books counteracts monolingualism. The book is the place of difference and plurality. It breaks down the fundamentalist passion for ignorance.

On the one hand, we have the temptation of the wall – 'one single people', 'one single language' – and on the other, we have the unique resistance of the book, which contains the foreign plurality of languages. The book is a figure of openness. It is the sea as opposed to a wall. And the sea unites many countries, territories, races, languages. To read a book is always to experience democracy, pluralism, the death of monolingualism, to encounter other languages.[10] In this sense, the struggle against the ignorance of fundamentalism coincides with the struggle for the freedom of the book, as that ignorance would like to substitute the plurality of languages with the mortal aberration of the single language, the 'only language', the language of prejudice that denies the existence of all other languages because they are foreign.

An Anecdote about Freud

In civilized life, inclusion prevails over exclusion, welcoming over rejection, mediation over conflict. From a psychoanalytic perspective, adequately healthy mental activity always occurs through plastic integration and not rigid division. For Bollas this is the principle for the function of a 'democratic mind' or a 'democratic state of mind' founded on the action of 'vacillation' rather than one of immediate and rigid resolution:

> The democratic mind [. . .] aims to hold and tolerate all its differing elements so that nothing is eliminated. Invested with attending to all parts, the democratic process makes use of vacillation as a mental activity devoted to moving back and forth between all parts of a mind.[11]

An anecdote from Freud's life might help us better understand this definition.[12] At a point when he was already famous and widely recognized as the father of psychoanalysis, Freud gave a public lecture in a prestigious location, but was constantly interrupted by a man in the hall. After several requests to temper his behaviour, the man was removed. But not even this was enough to calm him, and he continued to do his best to disrupt the great psychoanalyst's lecture from outside. Eventually, the member of staff responsible for the conference whispered to Freud that it had become necessary to call the police. At that point, however, Freud decided not to do this, choosing instead to ask the man to return to the hall and hear what he had to say. This gesture not only reveals Freud's profound humanity (his civility), but also psychoanalysis' basic aim: not to segregate, not to exclude, not to remove the word but to give it to the person who has been excluded.

Essentially, what is psychoanalysis if not a kind of internal parliament in which different languages, or 'instances' (as, more appropriately, Freud himself would say), that make up the subject have the possibility of freely expressing themselves without censure or prohibition? And this episode, of course, went on to become a text in Freud's theory, in which the unconscious itself is compared to a stranger who disturbs the 'conference' held in our Ego, one we must allow to enter, rather than excluding it in the way a process of repression would do.[13] Psychoanalysis is a science of boundaries that values the experience of friendship and hospitality with the internal stranger. This is, as we have seen, the plastic and porous nature of the border as recognized by Bion.

In Praise of Ignorance

There is, however, a positive form of ignorance, defined by Nicola Cusano as 'learned ignorance'. It is not ignorance as a pretext for possessing the truth, but as a motor behind the search for truth. This implies that, for this positive form of ignorance, truth is not seen as someone's possession but rather as the result of continual research. It is ignorance as 'episte-mophilic instinct', in the words of Melanie Klein. The urge for knowledge is a libidinal need, like eating or having sex. In this case, ignorance does not stand in the way of knowledge, but encourages it. It demonstrates how not knowing is at the basis of all knowledge. It is not ignorance as an assumption of possessing a consolidated knowledge, but the desire to know that which eludes the knowledge we already have.

For this kind of 'ignorance', the question is worth more than any answer, because knowledge cannot be treated as a posses-sion but must instead circulate, be passed on. 'Knowledge', Don Milani wrote in his *Letter to a School Teacher*, 'is useful only if it is shared.' With the necessary addition that a teacher is no such thing if they do not engage in this activity of transmission: 'Only those who have no cultural interest when they are alone may call themselves a teacher'.[14] This is the profound difference between explaining and trivializing: explaining means only saying that which is essential, doing without the superfluous so that the essential can reach the greatest number of people, while trivializing means saying that which is superfluous and doing away with the essential. However, whilst the teacher makes every effort to circulate knowledge in order to chip away at the fundamentalist consolidation of ignorance, they are well aware that they could never know everything, they know that no one can hold all knowledge. And this awareness is in no way an obstacle to my quest for knowledge, rather it makes it possible. This is something that we also find in the myth of Genesis: only the impossibility of accessing God's knowledge, of knowing *everything* there is to know, makes the quest for knowledge possible.

The desire to know presupposes that the field of knowledge can never be exhaustively circumscribed, because there is always something that eludes knowledge, because the order of knowledge is not a totality but a 'not-everything'. We cannot know everything there is to know. No knowledge can appropriate for itself the mystery of life. This would be like reducing the beauty of the flame down to the simple physical phenomenon of wood combusting.

4

Fanaticism

The loss of racial purity ruins the fortunes of a race for ever;
it continues to sink lower and lower in mankind (and its
consequences can never be expelled again from body and mind).

Adolf Hitler, *Mein Kampf* (*My Struggle*)[1]

The Power of a Flag

In a speech to the German youth, Hitler praises attachment to
the flag of Greater Germany. His words enflame, seduce, con-
quer. The flag offers an ideal of a compact, everlasting, eternal
identity to the 'natural' insecurity of youth. A solid ideological
platform that saves us from getting lost, from bewilderment.
Hitler's speech resonates, because it demonstrates how the ideal
of the Aryan race gives an exalted sense of belonging that not
even death can erode.

In direct antagonism to the perennially exiled condition of
the Jewish people, but more generally, to human fragility, the
Führer invokes the flag as an indestructible symbol of identity.
Identification with the flag saves us from our lack and our vulnerability: 'saves us from the nothingness', Hitler affirms sug-
gestively. It is no coincidence that the more recent phenomenon

of Muslim radicalization highlights not so much the need for social redemption, but that of roots, of finding a solid identity, of belonging to a group that will not abandon us.

The Fanatical Phantom of Purity

Freud believes the mass offers a solid identity because it is acephalous, without a head, 'mindless' as Bion would say. Being in the mass, identifying with the mass, means participating in a collective hypnosis that brings about regression and a loss of critical judgement in exchange for feeling protected and bonded within one large collective body. In Nazism, the fanaticism was both nationalist and racist. Blood and soil are, by no means accidentally, its most powerful symbols. The purity of the Aryan race is its primary obsession. In this way, Nazism reflects the spirit that links all types of fundamentalism: *the exaltation of one's own purity* (and moral superiority) *against the poison of the Other's impurity* (their moral inferiority).

That which is different is always described as *deformed*, both morally and physically. The phantom of purity makes its spectral return in every form of fundamentalist ideology. If purity coincides with identity and impurity with difference, then purity embodies the exemplary way to be in the innocent eyes of a child. For this reason, fundamentalisms of all kinds exalt youth as the locus of absolute adhesion to the Cause. The twentieth century rounded up its children, dressing them up as little soldiers of the Cause. Mature thought can only corrupt the natural courage of the innocent. The terrorists of ISIS exalt the fanatical ideal of purity, transforming children into killers and deranged preachers. In the psychology of the terrorist, dedication to the Cause, to the point of sacrificing one's own life, is absolute. It is a wholesale, adhesive identification that allows no waste. The terrorist always acts in the name of what is good and of doing good. In consecrating their own life to the good of the Cause, no limit is placed on the exercise of evil. This is the human and political tragedy of all totalitarianism: carrying out evil in the name of good perfectly justifies the need for evil. For this reason, there is no longer a limit to the evil that can be carried out if it is done in the supreme name of that which is good.

The phantom of the terrorist's purity eradicates any doubt or uncertainty. Its seduction can prove irresistible: the truth is always on our side, it belongs to us, it is ours. The disconcerting figure of the child who, guided by Islamic terrorists, becomes the executioner of the 'infidels' provides further (horrifying) proof of this analysis. Their hand does not falter, they show no fragility, they know no uncertainty, they have no need to move towards another hand, as the insecure hand of a child usually does. This hand, the hand of the child chosen for the ferocious, solemn task of executioner, of the one who brings vengeance to the infidels, is the most wicked incarnation of innocence placed at the blind service of the Cause. The phantom of purity seems to have found its ideal player.

We must never forget that many Islamic terrorists are teenagers, young people, sometimes children, those who martyr themselves killing themselves and others in the name of the cause are lives who have not reached adulthood, who have not yet built a family. This is not a simple sociological cliché that should put our consciences at rest, as in 'they are young and don't know what they are doing'. Rather, the child can show much less mercy than an adult because they have not yet symbolically metabolized the authentic sense of alterity. Their world is the world of their parents, their family, the group to which they belong. Their satisfaction depends on satisfying the expectations of the adults they love and in whom they have blind faith. They are entirely assimilated by the environment in which they live. The power of critical thought has not yet corrupted (as happens in adolescence) their life. They are a knight of faith in the Other.

This is why their obedience can be acritical, pure, absolute. It is precisely this 'virtue' that pushes the paedophile in search of children: to find a body entirely at their disposal, without limits, inhibitions, uncertainty. To find someone who trusts them blindly, who will abandon their own body to his. This is the perverse-paedophilic heart of the phantom of purity.

We might ask ourselves, is paedophilia intrinsic to all totalitarian 'education'? Isn't all totalitarian 'education' based on brainwashing that leaves no space for freedom in our children? The child carries with them a fundamentalist soul because they believe entirely in their Other, they believe in their flag, in their ideals, they live to satisfy the Other in whom they have total faith. Can a child really be said to be a criminal? Could we have seen young Hitler's eyes and guessed at his bloody destiny? Could we really see the cynical, exalted sneer of the killer in the masked face of the little ISIS executioner? Wouldn't it be more correct to say that it is the adults who always make children (thanks to their faith in the Other) the passive tool of their own enjoyment? Isn't this the paedophilic nucleus at the heart of every totalitarian education?

It is without doubt that the most terrible crime is that of subjugating the life of those who trust us to protect them. If the absolute declaration of innocence and purity has a paranoid aspect in adults, it is because it always attributes the responsibility for the evil to the Other. In children, this innocence and purity can become atrocious because they lack authentic altruistic thought, a true awareness of the Other. They can only do the religious bidding of their masters. The child maliciously elevated to the role of executioner cannot know the torment of guilt or forgiveness, and for this reason, they lend themselves to being even more merciless than their manipulators (if this is possible): the executioner who, in their innocence and purity, ends up justifying a crime it is impossible to justify.

The recurring question when it comes to the reasons for terroristic violence in general is the same one we ask when faced with the totalitarian barbarity of the Shoah: how was it possible? Why did they do it? And, most of all, are these cruel, merciless assassins, deprived of any *pietas*, still human? Do they still belong to the human race?

The spirit of terrorism is founded on total submission and the surrendering of insidious freedom. Nevertheless, in their blind submission to the Cause, they are supposedly exercising their supreme freedom. This is the point that links a young terrorist to the anorexic: subjugation to an inflexible Ideal is the highest form of freedom. As Camus says, the sacrifice of one's life in the name of a Cause contains the right to one's own salvation. This is the awful phantom that belongs to all pathological forms of sacrificial religiosity. The reward awaiting those who sacrifice their own lives is always overabundant: if this life is nothing, the next one will finally bring you fulfilment. These young people's desire to kill is mixed with their desire to die. This is the dynamic of martyrdom that, in this case however, implies not only their only death (as we see with Antigone), but that of innocent victims.

But is killing innocent victims whilst you kill yourself the manifestation of a narcissistic lack or its crazed amplification? Is a terrorist really a slave to their Cause or are they actually using the Cause to transform their life from an insignificant void into that of a heroic executioner sent by God? The Islamic sanctification of martyrdom, unlike the Christian one, requires active and militant struggle against the infidel. It is not limited to the passive consignment of the self to sacrifice.

For Marco Belpoliti, the suicidal urge can only be understood within a 'paradigm of the victim': to become a victim, to sacrifice oneself for the Cause ennobles one's own life in the eyes of the community to which one belongs.[2] Death is not that which limits our life, reminding us of our extreme insufficiency and vulnerability, but becomes the occasion for its maximum exaltation: a 'proof of self-love', a 'direct relationship with God' that 'allows a kind of absolute enjoyment'.[3]

Escape from Freedom

After Freud, Reich and Fromm delved deep into the subject of the mass psychology found in fascism and the phenomenon of fanaticism. Their fundamental premise is that the fanatical euphoria of the masses circumvents the ethical responsibility required by individuals to take on the weighty burden of their own freedom.

In dark, uncertain times, the urge to take refuge in a master's hands can be irresistible. To masochistically entrust yourself to a sadistic boss means you can be freed from the anxiety of freedom. It means, as Fromm explains very clearly, escaping from freedom.[4] This is the central paradox of the securitarian drive highlighted by these studies: human beings may prefer chains to freedom if it means avoiding the heady responsibility of choice. It is no surprise that Reich, in his analysis of the psychology of fascism, insisted that the true enigma of fascist totalitarianism did not lie in the passive subordination to the dictatorship by the masses.[5] Rather, Reich believed, it lay in the disconcerting existence of the masses' active desire for fascism. In questioning the 'eternal' (as Umberto Eco would put it) dimension of fascism.[6]

Indeed, there is a fascist quality to human desire which, in order to avoid taking on the burden of the ethical responsibility that comes with freedom, tends to create relationships of dependency and submission. This 'eternal' dimension of fascism locks on to the original urge behind the drive: to spit out, to push away, projecting the stranger that lives within us

onto the outside world. It is what leads us to suppress or segregate the intruder that accompanies us throughout our lives
like a shadow, like a heart of darkness. As Eco explains, all
fascism aims at eliminating the intruder, contamination, pluralism, difference, any infection of alterity, to abolish the restless
democratic space. Every fascism is, in fact, segregationist, and
all segregationism is fascist.

To adhere fanatically to the Cause offers the maximum solid-
ification of identity, activating processes for evacuating and
expelling the intruder. Critical thought is lost as obedience to
the Cause comes to dominate. This is the religious essence of all
fanaticism: multitudes can be killed in God's name. But fanaticism also means the cancelling out of everything that is viewed
as negative: illness, poverty, vulnerability, the Jewish people,
women, imperfection, death, all in the name of a glorious future.
The mirage of all fanaticism is that we are offered a future
without lack, one in which nothing is impossible, in exchange
for absolute obedience. This is its fundamental euphoria, its
basic maniacal nature. But this euphoria is founded on the total
cessation of one's own liberty. According to Fromm, at the
basis of all fanaticism is the belief in a 'higher power outside of
the individual, toward which the individual can do nothing but
submit'.[7] This is the tendency of that which Fromm – following
the sociology research developed at the heart of the Frankfurt
School by Adorno and Horkheimer – defined as the 'authoritarian character'. It is the idolatrous aspect of every fanaticism:
to experience the relationship with the higher power as one of
'absolute dependence'.[8]

The Inhumane Primacy of the Idea

As Hannah Arendt insists, all totalitarianism is founded on the primacy of the universal Idea, rather than the irregular singularity of life. Fanaticism arms us, authorizes evil, unleashes violence in the name of absolute Good. Even the most ferocious violence can be justified in the name of the inhumane nature of the Cause, even coming to signify crazed redemption. The fanatic who kills in the name of the Cause annihilates life in the name of the Idea: of Race, History, People, Greater Germany, God, Class Struggle. It is always the Idea that authorizes mortal violence, or as Arendt states, the unadulterated use of 'terror'.

In the eyes of Nazi fanaticism, the Jewish people, Communists, homosexuals, liberals, the middle classes, Christians are not simply social or anthropological figures, but incarnations of Evil and, as such, must be ripped up and exterminated. It is the same logic that inspires any violent act carried out in the name of an identification with the absolute purity of the Cause. For this reason, Arendt reminds us that all ideology would like to bend 'experience' – the plural and uniquely irreducible lives of human beings – to a certain idea of Human and humanity, forgetting that it is not the Human in general, but always unique humans who walk the earth.

Terror, on the other hand, cancels out the plurality of faces and lives – the unique existence of human beings – in order to carry out the necessary and universal plan of the Idea.[9] It sacrifices the subject's own name to the abstract Ideal of the Cause. It is in the name of this Ideal that the Red Brigade militant killed

Aldo Moro, not just as a political adversary, but as a brother who had betrayed, a deserter, a villain, someone not worthy of the shared Cause, who failed to disavow himself in the name of the Ideal. It is no coincidence that more terrible and radical interpreters of the Law have historically been heretics, the first transgressors of the Law.

In psychoanalysis, this is the vicious cycle that characterizes the bloody paradox of the Super-Ego. The entanglement of its Kantian face with its Sadist one; of the command to obey ('You must!') with that of enjoyment ('Enjoy!'); of the inhumane and rigorous application of the Law (Kant) with its libertine transgression (Sade). This is what enables heretics to terrifyingly transform themselves into the most implacable traditionalists in the blink of an eye. In the same way, idealist fanatics who heroically sacrifice their lives in the name of the Cause of freedom and equality can show themselves to be unhesitating killers.

The Universal and the Particular

Fanaticism always implies the annihilation of memory. The consigning of the past to oblivion, reducing it to an abandoned cemetery. It pursues the ideal of a glorious future with euphoric determination (the transcendent world of religions; the dictatorship of the proletariat; the dominion of the Aryan race and so on), to which historic time must submit. All imperfection – illness, death, poverty, loneliness – is destined to be overcome. The universal hypnotizes the particular, whilst, at the same time, having to redeem it. This, according to Arendt, is the true root of all totalitarianism. Fanaticism aims to forget the individual life in the name of the universal Idea of the Cause. As a consequence, politics is transformed into religion, cancelling out history and the faces of individuals in the name of the abstract universal that is the Cause.

But it is precisely this face of all individuals that every lexicon of civility must protect: to preserve the irreplaceable and concrete nature of the particular in the face of the abstract motives of the universal. This is a subject that inspired the highly intense pages Philip Roth dedicated to the juxtaposition of literature and politics:

> Politics is the great generalizer [. . .] and literature the great particularizer, and not only are they in an inverse relationship to each other – they are in an *antagonistic* relationship. To politics, literature is decadent, soft, irrelevant, boring, wrongheaded, dull, something that makes no sense and that really oughtn't to be. Why? Because the particularizing impulse *is* literature. How can you be an artist and renounce the nuance? But how can you be a politician and *allow* the nuance? As an artist the nuance is your *task*. Your task is *not* to simplify. [. . .]. Not to erase the contradiction, not to deny the contradiction, but to see where, within the contradiction, lies the tormented human being. To allow for the chaos, to let it in. You *must* let it in. Otherwise you produce propaganda, if not for a political party, a political movement, then stupid propaganda for life itself – for life as it might itself prefer to be publicized. [. . .] Generalizing suffering: there is Communism. Particularizing suffering: there is literature. In that polarity is the

antagonism. Keeping the particular alive in a simplifying, generalizing world – that's where the battle is joined. You do not have to write to legitimize Communism, and you do not have to write to legitimize capitalism. You are out of both.[10]

In these pages we see the heterogeneity of the particular and the universal highlighted through the juxtaposition of literature (particular) and politics (universal). At play here is the heterogeneity of the face (ethics) and the multitude (politics). The American author defines literature here in the same way Lacan once defined psychoanalysis, as a 'science of the particular'.[11] While politics reasons using universal principles, numbers, algorithms, power relations, processes and so on, literature – like psychoanalysis – focuses on the detail, even those dimensions of the particular that are worthless, contradictory, accidental, contingent. If politics concerns itself with generalization, with order, with propaganda, with necessity and higher laws, then literature's thoughts are of detail, nuance, suffering, the particular and its chaos.

The Spirit of Sacrifice

Apology for the Cause implies the extreme sacrifice of individual life. Its principle is the same as the spirit of sacrifice. It is no coincidence that in *Mein Kampf*, Hitler praises the spirit of sacrifice as a specifically Aryan virtue, given they are superior beings, 'a superior race, carrier of human civilisation', 'the Prometheus of humanity':

In giving up one's own life for the existence of the community lies the crowning of all will to sacrifice [. . .] Now the basic disposition out of which such an activity grows we call idealism, to distinguish it from egoism. By this we understand only the individual's ability to sacrifice himself for the community, for his fellow citizens.[12]

While the middle-class Ego would defend its pitiful survival as its supreme value, the Aryan lives their life subjugating its particular to the universal of the Idea. They intrepidly throw their lives into the struggle, obeying the absolute of the Cause to which they heroically sacrifice their lives. The Aryan voluntarily submits themselves to the idea of the Cause. They are ready to sacrifice their unique existence without hesitation. In Hitler's eyes, this is the spirit of sacrifice that makes the German people stand out. As Fromm clearly states, placing themselves at the service of the Cause, sacrificing their own life in the name of an absolute Ideal (the supremacy of the Aryan race) that removes all value from the individual life, is not simply a passively masochistic position.[13] In the Aryan spirit of sacrifice, the masochism of submission is flipped, becoming its opposite – sadism – because it is through this self-sacrifice that the Aryan (like the Islamist suicide bomber or the Red terrorist) can earn the right to assimilate themselves with God, to elevate themselves to the absolute of the Cause. To kill in the name of God, Race, History, a People is, in other words, the sadistic prize for one's masochistic submission. Nevertheless, it is always the idea of the Cause that arms the killer, who by acting in the name of absolute Good can, as we have seen, justify any atrocity.

This is why the Aryan must earn back the purity of their blood, freeing themselves from that 'mixing of blood' that lies at the basis of all decadence. It is this earned purity of one's own being that allows them to wipe impurity from the face of the earth.

5

Freedom

Only when incomplete can democracy remain such.

Roberto Esposito, *Dieci pensieri sulla politica*
(*Ten Thoughts of Politics*)

The Urge to Freedom

Freedom is a, if not *the*, fundamental word for any lexicon of civility. Human life is not only a request for belonging, but also a demand for freedom, a desire to wander. However, freedom is not simply an experience of liberation, affirmation of the uniqueness of our own lives, but it is also, paradoxically, a 'sentence'. Human beings are, as Sartre said, 'condemned to be free'.[1] Human existence is, as such, always condemned to freedom.

Unlike the animal kingdom, where the law of instinct dominates unequivocally, causing reactive behaviour that is genetically fixed and that does not involve the ethical dimension of choice, for the human world, the chain of drives is suspended, interrupted, traumatized. As a result, the drive, as opposed to instinct, is freer to 'choose' ways of satisfying itself that are not necessarily already established within the unambiguous framework of drive. Thought, fantasy, imagination, eroticism all flow from this freedom from drive, making different forms of satisfaction possible outside that rigid framework.

This means that we can never free ourselves from freedom, that if we are free it is not because we chose to be, but because we were thrown into it, forced, bound, chained to freedom. In fact, no one can choose for us, and even when we decide to submit ourselves entirely to a master, when we decide to escape from freedom, it is always our own free choice to do so, an irreducible manifestation of our freedom.

For this reason, as it is a sentence, a bond, freedom is the chosen locus of anxiety when faced with the dilemma of choice. I cannot free myself from the responsibility of the choice, I cannot escape its burden. Even if I choose not to choose, this option will always remain the expression of a unique choice.[2] This is why Sartre states that we are all always 'alone and without excuse'.[3] This is why freedom is not simply a breeze, a walk in the park, but always implies the ambiguous temptation of its denial, the temptation to do away with freedom. We could even say that human life is lacerated by freedom. *It is an aspiration to freedom and, at the same time, an anxiety when faced with freedom.* It is the urge to be radically free, and at the same time, the urge to avoid the vertigo freedom implies, to sabotage one's own freedom. With regard to this last tendency, Nietzsche writes about feeling 'homesick for the land', an affliction experienced by even the greatest travellers.[4] In the midst of the sea's infinite horizon, we not only experience the intoxication of freedom, the expansion of horizons, the encounter with the infinite, but, as Nietzsche reminds us, we are always also ambushed by feeling 'homesick for the land', for land, for our home. This means that *freedom can never be entirely dissociated from the anxiety it causes.*

Freud states that this anxiety is behind the securitarian drive, the drive that, rather than urging life on, holds it back, appealing to the self-preservation of our own identity. As we have seen, this drive, as fundamental as the erotic, tends to form ever larger groups, expanding its radius of action and the horizons of the world.

In *Escape from Freedom*, Fromm distinguishes between 'freedom from' and 'freedom to'.[5] The first is an immature form of freedom that resembles simple opposition, as we see (for example) in adolescence, when the child claims a freedom that is only a freedom 'from', that is, from the varyingly rigid rules their family or school impose. This freedom – the 'freedom from' – maintains a bond of dependence with the people who have taken care of the child's life. As such, the subject that declares themselves free can, nevertheless, always maintain the 'primary' nature of their most profound ties. This is a freedom that can always return to the arms of those from whom the subject has separated themselves. In this sense it is an incomplete form of freedom and of the process of individualization. Conversely, 'freedom to' is the complete form of freedom, one which implies that a process of individualization has taken place.

To clarify this differentiation, Fromm refers to the biblical tale of the Garden of Eden. The freedom enjoyed by Adam and Eve before the act of transgression was only an incomplete form of liberty. They lived lost in the harmonious immediacy of nature. It is only their transgression of the rule forbidding them from accessing the tree of knowledge that interrupts this fusion without difference. In this act of disobedience Fromm reads the first manifestation of human freedom.[6] The suffering that comes from this act – expulsion from the Garden of Eden – demonstrates that 'freedom from' God is not yet the same as the self-affirming freedom of the subject, with their full 'freedom to' exist autonomously. It is only the definitive severing of this relationship that allows for the passage from 'freedom from' to 'freedom to'. But the 'freedom from' can never in itself ensure a passage to 'freedom to'. This means that the necessary liberation from constrictions is not yet the same as the complete exercise of freedom.

The Sado-Masochistic Bond

As we have seen, human beings can be terrorized by freedom. In *Escape from Freedom*, Fromm explains the existence of 'mechanisms of escape'[7] that activate when the subject faces experiences of loss or solitude that they cannot control. So the tendency to return to those primary bonds of dependence is accentuated and prejudices the affirmation of one's own freedom.

If separation from those primary bonds, through a 'process of individualization', plunges life into uncertainty, the tendency will be to compensate for this uncertainty through the restoration of bonds of dependence that are similar to the primary ones, bonds that are capable of excluding any experience of separation and freedom. In this sense, this is a mechanism for an escape from freedom.

This is a paradox that Spinoza had already highlighted: a human can love their chains, their enslavement, more than their freedom. This is what lies at the heart of the securitarian drive. This drive can, in turn, be perverted through sado-masochistic bonds. In these bonds, the subject can feed the illusion that the Other is able to give them that consistency of being they feel they lack. Instead of subjectivizing their lack, and completing their process of individualization, it becomes easier for them to meld with an Other who shows they are able to offer solidity and guidance through this fusion. Masochistic dependency on the sadist's power creates a strong bond that cancels out both the experience of lack and that of freedom. In the masochist, this is made entirely clear by the way in which they consign themselves entirely and passively to a 'magical helper' who must guarantee their life by removing from it the responsibility of choice.[8] Better fusion and dependency on the Other than the boundless experience of freedom.

If the sexual perversion of masochistic behaviour consists of gaining pleasure from pain, at play in the masochistic bond is not a simple sexual fantasy, but a positioning of the subject with regard to the Other which is characterized by ceding the subject's own subjectivity, by placing themselves like clay to be moulded in the hands of the Other. The payoff of this position lies in the freedom from the anxiety of solitude and choice. By placing their entire existence in the hands of the Other, the masochist escapes the anxiety-making sensation of having been abandoned that accompanies their life.

Bonds that are deprived of freedom are like a form of torture that one cannot, however, live without. Submission to the sadistic will of a master allows us to '*get rid of the burden of freedom*'.⁹ We can see this in dramatic fashion in a film by Matteo Garrone, *Primo amore* (*First Love*, 2004), which tells of a woman forced to become anorexic by a sadistic man who becomes her lover, her master and her 'magical helper'. The anorexia in this tale is not a choice by the subject, but a perfectly perverse prison built by the man. The woman renounces her freedom, not so much in exchange for love (which in this case does not exist), but for the intoxication she feels when she submits herself entirely to the will of the Other. This is absolute submission. Whilst the choice to be anorexic usually aims to separate the subject from the Other, proclaiming their own freedom, here we see its masochistic delivery to an Other who appears as a sadistic master.

In this case, as with all bonds that are profoundly sado-masochistic, the masochist's aim is not to enjoy the evil inflicted upon them by their sadistic master, but, as Fromm points out, it is, more profoundly, that of 'forget[ting] ourselves',¹⁰ of cancelling themselves out by fleeing any responsibility other than blind obedience.

The dependency, however, no matter how it might appear, is reciprocal. While the victim's dependency on their tormentor is entirely evident, it is also continually active in the master's relationship with their slave, albeit in a much less obvious way. This is something that we often see in action in pathological couples. When the masochistic subject finds the strength to rebel against the injustices meted out by the sadistic master, the latter is plunged into anxiety. Without the support of their servant, the master's life appears entirely meaningless.

In both cases (the sadist and the masochist) what we have is, therefore, a 'forgetting of one's own existence', a wholesale deliverance into the hands of the Other. This symbiosis trumps individualization; the inability to support one's own lack and solitude gives rise to a profound destructiveness. Lacan sees this as the quintessential religiosity of all bonds of dependency: the subject consigns themselves to the Other, transforming them into an idol. It is not religion (contrary to what Freud believed) that is a neurosis ('neurosis of humanity'), but it is neurosis itself, in its belief in an omnipotent Other and their 'permanent altruism' to which one's own desire can be entrusted, that reveals itself to be profoundly religious.[11]

We Never Live Alone

Freud believed that Civilization is built upon the forfeit of the individual and immediate satisfaction of the drive. If human beings have a drive to be asocial (as psychoanalysis insists on demonstrating, flying in the face of Aristotle's definition of humans as social animals), this coincides with the drive to search out their exclusive enjoyment, regardless of anyone else. The drive's agenda demands only its own autistic fulfilment. Conversely, civilization imposes a deferment of this satisfaction of drives, requiring its partial domestication. These two agendas – that of the drive and that of Civilization – are structurally opposed, destined to cause a conflict that excludes any ideal of harmonious reconstruction. This is what Freud called the 'discontent of civilization': the civilization of humans depends on the repression of the animal, its 'annihilation', as Kojève would say in Hegelian fashion.[12]

For Freud, the edification of Civilization demands the forfeit of the full satisfaction of the drive. This is a necessary symbolic sacrifice that makes community life possible. In this way, the Other is not only an external limit to my freedom, but that which reveals an impossibility within me: the impossibility of fully giving in to my drives. As Freud said, the Other is never missing from the mental life of the subject: individual psychology is a problematic real that we cannot avoid. But the existence of others should not be thought of as something that is added to my freedom at a later date, like a kind of extrinsic possession. It is not 'Me' and then the others; there is not my freedom on one side and that of the others on the other. My freedom always implies that of the others, it is never freedom without others. This is the case from the moment we are born. No one can choose their own parents or their social origins, but no one can exist without their parents or social origins. Human life carries with it the form of a 'being-with', of a life that is always connected to the Other.[13]

Freedom is not creating ourselves from nothing, making a name for ourselves, as the delirious people of the tower of Babel believed, but the possibility, as Sartre reiterates, of doing something with what has been done to us. It is not the option for self-affirmation without recognizing the social ties with which our lives have been and are tied. It is never self-generation. Sartre defines it as a 'small deviation',[14] and that 'deviation' allows us to subjectivize, to make our own, the starting conditions for our own lives, which we haven't yet chosen. To make, therefore, something of that which the Other has made of us. This is a clear way of defining the inheritance that makes us human: making our own that which we have received from the Other. If we cannot choose to be free, if we are 'condemned to freedom', if we cannot avoid having to make a choice and the irrevocable nature of its obligation, then we are also the continuing possibility for a transformation of the destiny decided for us by others into a new, unexpected adventure, as the path taken by Tara Westover shows us so powerfully.

Degeneration of Freedom

Freedom does not mean doing without others; any fantasy of self-generation is perverse. Instead, it means recognizing our dependency on others. Indeed, when freedom is posited as absolute, as contrary to human Law, when the only Law possible is the Law without Law of freedom, we find ourselves faced with a purely perverse version of freedom. It is a freedom that, by denying any symbolic form of the Law, places itself above the Law. This is freedom as pure free will, predation, will to power, that experiences anything that limits its natural expansion as an imposition. It is a libertine version of freedom that found its perfect embodiment in the Marquis de Sade. It is freedom as the Law of enjoyment without limits, which becomes the only possible form of the Law.[15] It is not freedom as a simple transgression of the Law, but as a new (inhumane) Law that transcends (human) Law. The perverse hates the Law because it cannot bear that a Law could have the right to restrain its own absolute freedom, which it erroneously considers to be the only plausible form of the Law.

This perverse version of freedom ends up unravelling the freedom of a community. An irreducible antagonism makes the neo-libertine declination of freedom irreconcilable with the democratic life of the community. Though this perverse version of freedom ends up coinciding with the headless nature of drive, politics (in the highest sense of the term) should instead return freedom to the community. But freedom could, then, only be imagined as an individual appeal to one's own civil responsibility. This is why Aristotle rightly held politics to be the most noble of all arts. Politics serves the life of the *polis*, it pulls together the individual differences, making possible their complex convergence.

Unlike the libertine version of freedom that refuses any limit, politics is the art that works on the sidelines to incessantly create and re-create the possible conditions for a community. But this work of creation–re-creation excludes fusion outright, it rejects the idea of a communion that abolishes differences in the indistinct homogeneity of a single body and single language. The foundation of the community cannot help but be the responsibility of 'one for one', of the individual who generates the necessarily plural possibility of the community.

This unique foundation is front and centre in a wonderful scene from Roberto Andò's 2013 film *Viva la libertà* (*Long Live Freedom*) when, during an electoral assembly, the orator, played by a formidable Toni Servillo, who surprises the audience by reciting a poem by Brecht, does not address an anonymous mass, as usually occurs, but addresses his unique partner in conversation in the crowd, addressing them using the singular you, 'tu!'

The civil passion of politics, if we do not want to forget life, must be maintained through a constant return to 'one for one'. A community must not forget the nature of individual freedom, if it is to avoid falling into a dictatorial exercise of power. This does not elevate freedom to a cornerstone of community, but rather is a recognition that there is no chance for democratic community without welcoming the plurality of individuality. This does not confuse community with communion, but recognizes that it is precisely in the impossibility of this confusion that we can find the individual foundation of every community.[16] In the words of Elvio Fachinelli, it means making possible not so much a community of equals (which would be fatally repressive of plural individuality), but 'a relationship of equality founded among those who are not the same'.[17]

Populism as an Incestuous Deviation of Democracy

The 'one for one' of those who are 'not the same' is not the same as the 'one equals one' found in populist rhetoric. Populism is an illness of democracy, a symptomatic signal of its dangerously incestuous tendency.

The premise for this diagnosis is populism's radical aversion to politics as an art crafted from the multiple interests and subjects present in life in the *polis*. Populists have mostly decided to opt for the suppression of any kind of compromise in the name of the general will of the people or citizens. A propagandistic lexicon overwhelms the political, and usurps that difficult task of mediation between and composition of the city's particular interests, pursuing electoral consensus by any means necessary.

The necessarily lengthy political thought process (as Enrico Berlinguer reminded us) is crushed by the immediacy of the search for consensus above all else. Politics itself is seen as a betrayal of the people rather than the chosen place for their representation. Instead, the sovereignty of the people is demagogically brandished in the face of the representative nature of democracy and its symbolic laws.

The dogmatic premise is false and abstract. The people, whether a generic or non-existent entity, is the same as the Good. Criticism of privilege, revolt against the ruling classes, the refusal of all symbols of power strengthen this demagogical equivalence. The rhetoric of propaganda takes the place of critical reflection.

Here, we cannot help but recall Plato's famous image in which the orator, a populist demagogue, is compared to the cakemaker who offers a group of sick children a cure consisting of the unlimited consumption of sweets and all kinds of delicious treats. His little patients obviously find this diet much more welcome and credible than that of the healthy diet proposed by a stern but thorough doctor.

The anti-political crusade of populism does not realize that it is throwing the baby out with the bathwater. The war on politics and its corruption ends up dragging us towards improvisation and isolation, confining discourse to a blind rhetoric of anti-institutionalism. This is why attacks on the symbols of democracy (such as that on the Italian parliament at the time of the first great advance made by the Five Star Movement) are not simply aesthetic, but the cipher of the fundamentally anti-institutional nature of all populism. Social envy is unleashed, striking the symbols of democracy and countering the logic of merit with that of the levelling of all difference, with the dissolution of representation, scientific expertise, the principle of delegation, while elevating the people to the role of social executioner.

Pauperism, statism, paternalism, rebellion, Peronism, anti-parliamentarism all run through every form of populism, incestuously espousing the securitarian drive that hates everything that would distract the drive from its self-preserving and, fatally, self-destructive urge.

The Poetry of Institutions

In the lexicon of civility, the area where freedom and community meet is in the existence of institutions, going against the populist rhetoric of 'one equals one' and its anti-institutional bent. According to Lacan, the primary aim of an institution is that of the 'reining in of jouissance' and the mindless urge of the drive.[18] But an institution is not simply a place where individual freedoms find their limit, their symbolic castration, to use a psychoanalytic term. Its function is not solely to regulate individual enjoyment. According to Pasolini, every institution always carries within it something 'moving' and 'mysterious'; it carries with it the mystery of coming together, the miracle of a community that is not founded on what we have in common but on each person's uniqueness, their unique differences:

> Beautiful fucking souls, why else would the
> two Kennedy brothers die, if not
> for an *institution*? And why else, if not for an *institution*,
> will so many small, sublime Vietcong perish?
> Because institutions are moving: and men do not know
> how to recognize themselves if not in them.
> They are what humbly make them brothers.
> There is something mysterious in institutions
> – the only form of life and a simple model for humanity –
> and the mystery of the individual is nothing by comparison.[19]

What is the poet telling us here? Careful not to spit on your fathers and mothers. Careful, 'beautiful fucking souls', not to declare your freedom in opposition to the existence of the institutions that *are* our fathers and mothers. If there is something 'moving' and 'mysterious' in institutions, something capable of outshining the miracle of individual life, we should look for it in the profound bond between freedom and responsibility, between history and future, between individual life and collective life, between Law and desire, between provenance and

destination. This is why Pasolini invites the younger generations not to desert politics but to participate in them, militantly.

The only thing people remember from his famous poem enti-
tled 'Il Pci ai giovani!' ('The Italian Communist Party to the
Youth!'), written in 1968 after the clash between students and
police known as the Battle of Valle Giulia, is the 'reactionary'
tone with which the poet takes the side of the police against the
young protestors. He states that he stands with the children of
the proletariat and not the children of the middle classes, and
that he prefers the 'poor' to the 'rich'. This, the *pars destruens*
of this text, has, unfortunately, completely obscured the *pars
construens*. The latter is actually introduced in the poem when
Pasolini posits himself as the symbolic father of this generation
of children, reminding them not to waste time: 'You are late,
children.'[20] In the poem's final verses, his appeal is repeated,
becoming powerful and crystal clear. The poet speaks to the
young protestors directly, inviting them to bravely participate
in the life of the *polis*. He speaks to the protagonists of 1968 to
encourage them to behave like my Telemachus:[21]

> But go instead, children, and assail Federations!
> Go and invade the cells!
> Go and occupy the offices
> of the Central Committee! Go, go
> and set up camp in Via delle Botteghe Oscure![22]

This appeal to his 'children' is aimed at setting life in motion,
not against the institutions but for them. It is no coincidence

that Pasolini asks them to go and occupy the headquarters of the former Italian Communist Party, to take responsibility for its direction. Institutions are not an obstacle to freedom, but should be its most accomplished symbolic translation. Nevertheless, institutions do not need only strength, but also poetry. The task of a lexicon of civility worthy of that name is that of bringing the institutions as close as possible to poetry. Not impersonal, grey machines, anonymous devices, places of alienation, but 'mysterious' and 'moving' dimensions where we achieve the miracle of life together. It is as if Pasolini is telling us, until this can happen, we must have the courage to introduce a new word.

In an article from 28 September 1968, published in the magazine *Tempo*, Pasolini writes that the ideals of hope and faith without that of charity have inflamed the world, but they have failed to transform it in a generative way. Hope and faith, when deprived of the word 'charity', have paradoxically justified humanity's worst crimes in the name of a glorious future that did not recognize the irreducible singularity of life.

It therefore becomes necessary to add a third word to understand the immanent poetry of institutions, and their 'moving' and 'mysterious' nature. Strictly speaking, this word does not belong to the political lexicon, but to that of Christian culture; more precisely, the lexicon of Paul of Tarsus. It is the word 'charity', which we can also translate (following Paul's teaching) with the word 'love'.[23] Without charity, without love, faith and hope are not only unthinkable, but even appear 'monstrous':

Charity – this mysterious and neglected thing – unlike faith and hope, which are so clear and so commonly used, is indispensable for those two very things. In fact, charity can exist on its own, while faith and hope are unthinkable without charity, and not just unthinkable, but *monstrous*.[24]

The mystery of the institutions – their poetry – should be that of binding charity with hope and faith. Only in this way can the singularity of 'one for one' be respected and not annihilated by the universal fury of ideology. A Law without forgiveness is inhumane, as is an institution without love.

Notes

Introduction

1 I recently developed an in-depth clinical reflection on these themes in my book *Le nuove melanconie: Destini del desiderio nel tempo ipermoderno* (*The New Melancholies: Destinies of Desire in Hypermodern Times*), Raffaello Cortina, Milan 2019.

2 The content of my Family Lexicon can be found throughout several of my books, including *Cosa resta del padre? La paternità nell'epoca ipermoderna* (*What Remains of the Father? Fatherhood in Hypermodern Times*), Raffaello Cortina, Milan 2011; *The Telemachus Complex: Parents and Children after the Decline of the Father*, Polity, Cambridge 2019; *The Mother's Hands: Desire, Fantasy and the Inheritance of the Maternal*, Polity, Cambridge 2019; *The Son's Secret: From Oedipus to the Prodigal Son*, Polity, Cambridge 2020. My Lexicon on Love can be found in the book *The Enduring Kiss: Seven Short Lessons on Love*, Polity, Cambridge 2021.

3 See Homer, *The Odyssey*, I, 214–20.

1 The Border

1 See Wilfred R. Bion, *Learning from Experience*, Heinemann, London 1962.

2 Sigmund Freud, 'Formulations on Two Principles of Mental Functioning', in *The Complete Psychological Works of Sigmund Freud, Vol. XII*, Vintage, London 2001, p. 220, note 4.

3 I use this expression very freely. It is taken, alongside other content that is not entirely alien to what I do, from L. Binswanger, 'La proporzione antropologica' ('The Anthropological Proportion'), in *Essere nel mondo* (*Being in the World*), Astrolabio, Rome 1973, pp. 346–53.

4 Franz Kafka, 'The Great Wall of China', in *The Great Wall of China and Other Pieces*, Secker and Warburg, London 1946, p. 87.

5 For more on all of these themes, I direct you to Recalcati, *Le nuove melanconie* (*The New Melancholies*).

6 See Roberto Esposito, *Bíos: Biopolitics and Philosophy*, University of Minnesota Press, Minneapolis 2008.

7 Thomas Hobbes, *Leviathan*, Penguin, London 2017.

8 Franz Kafka, 'The Burrow', in *The Great Wall of China and Other Pieces*, Secker and Warburg, London 1946, pp. 48–80.

9 See Sigmund Freud, 'Lecture XXXI: Dissection of the Psychical Personality', in *The Complete Psychological Works of Sigmund Freud, Vol. XXII*, Vintage, London 2001, pp. 57–80.

10 See Sigmund Freud, 'Instincts and their Vicissitudes', in *The Complete Psychological Works of Sigmund Freud, Vol. XIV*, Vintage, London 2001, pp. 117–40.

11 Elias Canetti, *Crowds and Power*, Seabury Press, New York 1978, p. 17.

12 See Michel Foucault, *A History of Madness*, Routledge, Abingdon 2009.

13 See Franco Basaglia, *Scritti (Writings)*, Einaudi, Turin 1981, 2 vols.

14 See Jacques Lacan, 'Presentation on Psychical Causality', in *Écrits*, W. W. Norton, New York 2006, pp. 123–60.

15 Jacques Lacan, 'The Third', *The Lacanian Review: Get Real*, 7, spring 2019, pp. 83–112.

16 Jean-Luc Nancy, 'The Intruder', in *Corpus*, Fordham University Press, New York 2008, p. 167.

17 Homer, *The Odyssey*, VI, 199–203 and 206–10.

2 Hate

1 Jacques Lacan, *Freud's Papers on Technique 1953–1954. The Seminar of Jacques Lacan: Book I*, W. W. Norton, London 1991, p. 277.

2 See Freud, 'Instincts and their Vicissitudes', pp. 117–40.

3 Sigmund Freud, *The Neuro-Psychoses of Defence*, Read Books, Redditch 2013, p. 23.

4 Franco Fornari, *The Psychoanalysis of War*, Indiana University Press, Bloomington 1975.

5 See Lacan, *Freud's Papers on Technique 1953–1954*.

6 Mariangela Gualtieri, *Caino (Cain)*, Einaudi, Turin 2011, p. 43.

7 See Melanie Klein, *Envy and Gratitude and Other Works: 1946–1963*, Vintage, London 1997.

8 Albert Camus, *Caligula*, Editions Gallimard, ed. Pierre-Louis Rey, 1993 (1944), p. 171.

9 For more on Judas' jealous envy, please see my book *La notte del Getsemani* (*The Night in Gethsemani*), Einaudi, Turin 2019, pp. 47–53.

10 Jacques Lacan, *The Ethics of Psychoanalysis. The Seminar of Jacques Lacan: Book VII*, Routledge, Abingdon 2008, p. 293.

11 Dante, *Purgatorio*, XIII, 70–2, in *The Divine Comedy: Inferno, Purgatorio, Paradiso*, Penguin, London 2021. For more on these themes, see Carla Casagrande and Silvana Vecchio, *I sette vizi capitali: Storia dei peccati nel Medioevo* (*The Seven Deadly Sins: The History of Sin in the Middle Ages*), Einaudi, Turin 2000, pp. 36–53.

12 See Thomas Aquinas, *On Evil*, Oxford University Press, New York 2003, p. 336.

3 Ignorance

1 See Sigmund Freud, 'Group Psychology and the Analysis of the Ego', in *The Complete Psychological Works of Sigmund Freud, Vol. XVIII*, Vintage, London 2001, p. 124.

2 This anti-patriarchal version of the father is addressed in depth in Recalcati, *Cosa resta del padre?* (*What Remains of the Father?*), *The Telemachus Complex*, *The Mother's Hands* and *The Son's Secret*.

3 See Recalcati, *The Son's Secret* and *The Telemachus Complex*.

4 Tara Westover, *Educated*, Random House 2018, p. 9 (eBook).

5 Ibid., p. 31.

6 Ibid., p. 73.

7 Ibid., pp. 352 and 364.

8 Ibid., p. 77.

9 Genesis 11: 1–9.

10 I would refer you here to my book *A libro aperto: Una vita è i suoi libri* (*An Open Book: A Life and its Books*), Feltrinelli, Milan 2018.

11 See Christopher Bollas, *Meaning and Melancholia: Life in the Age of Bewilderment*, Routledge, Abingdon 2018, p. 18.

12 See Ernest Jones, *The Life and Work of Sigmund Freud*, Basic Books, New York 1974.

13 See Sigmund Freud, 'Five Lectures on Psychoanalysis', in *The Complete Psychological Works of Sigmund Freud, Vol. XI*, Vintage, London 2001, pp. 21–9.

14 Don Milani, *Scuola di Barbiana: Lettera a una professoressa* (*School of Barbiana: Letter to a School Teacher*), Libreria editrice fiorentina, Florence 1967, p. 110.

4 Fanaticism

1 Adolf Hitler, *My Struggle*, Hurst and Blackett, London 1933, p. 144.

2 See Marco Belpoliti, *Chi sono i terroristi suicidi* (*Who Are the Suicide Bombers?*), Guanda, Milan 2017.

3 Ibid., p. 59.

4 Erich Fromm, *Escape from Freedom*, Ishi Press, New York 2011.

5 Wilhelm Reich, *The Mass Psychology of Fascism*, Souvenir Press, London 1972.

6 See Umberto Eco, *Il fascismo eterno* (*Eternal Fascism*), La nave di Teseo, Milan 2018.

7 Fromm, *Escape from Freedom*, p. 170.

8 Ibid., p. 171.

9 Hannah Arendt, *The Origins of Totalitarianism*, Meridian Books, New York 1960, pp. 460–79.

10 Philip Roth, *I Married a Communist*, Vintage, London 2005, p. 223.

11 See Jacques Lacan, *The Function and Field of Speech and Language in Psychoanalysis*, in *Écrits*, W. W. Norton, New York 2006, p. 216.

12 See Hitler, *My Struggle*, p. 410.

13 See Fromm, *Escape from Freedom*.

5 Freedom

1 See Jean-Paul Sartre, *Existentialism Is a Humanism*, Yale University Press, New Haven 2007, p. 29.

2 In psychoanalysis, who makes the choice is never a given. Is the Ego making the choice or the Unconscious? The Unconscious could be an alibi that relieves us of the responsibility ('It wasn't me, it was him, it was the Id!'), or it can dilate the notion of responsibility. Freud even asked himself whether we are responsible for our dreams. See Sigmund Freud, 'Some Additional Notes on Dream Interpretation as a Whole', in *The Complete Psychological Works of Sigmund Freud, Vol. XIX*, Vintage, London 2001.

3 Sartre, *Existentialism Is a Humanism*, p. 29.

4 Friedrich Nietzsche, *The Gay Science*, Vintage, New York 1974, p. 201.

5 See Fromm, *Escape from Freedom*, pp. 24–39.

6 Ibid.

7 Ibid., pp. 157–230.

8 Ibid., pp. 174–7.

9 Ibid., p. 152.

10 Ibid., p. 151.

11 See Jacques Lacan, *Desire and Its Interpretation. The Seminar of Jacques Lacan: Book VI*, Polity, Cambridge 2021, pp. 451–2.

12 See Alexandre Kojève, *Introduction to the Reading of Hegel: Lectures on the Phenomenology of Spirit*, Cornell University Press, Ithaca 1980, p. 155.

13 It is no coincidence that Heidegger believes the 'being-with' to be a fundamental ontological structure for existence. See Martin Heidegger, *Being and Time*, Martino Fine Books, Eastford 2019. A radical and irrefutably important reconsideration of 'being-with' can be found in Jean-Luc Nancy, *Being Singular Plural*, Stanford University Press, Stanford 2000.

14 See Jean-Paul Sartre, *The Family Idiot: Gustave Flaubert, 1821 to 1857*, University of Chicago Press, Chicago 2019.

15 For more on this theme, I refer you to my book *L'uomo senza inconscio: Figure della nuova clinica psicoanalitica* (*The Man without an Unconscious: New Figures in Clinical Psychoanalysis*), Raffaello Cortina, Milan 2010.

16 See Nancy, *Being Singular Plural*, and Roberto Esposito, *Communitas: The Origin and Destiny of Community*, Stanford University Press, Stanford 2010.

17 Elvio Fachinelli, 'Quale autorità nella scuola?' ('Where is the Authority in Schools?'), in *Al cuore delle cose: Scritti politici (1967–1989)* (*At the Heart of Things: Political Writings (1967–1989)*), DeriveApprodi, Rome 2016, p. 55.

18 See Jacques Lacan, 'Address on Child Psychoses', *Hurly-Burly*, 8, October 2012, p. 272.

19 Pier Paolo Pasolini, *Trasumanar e organizzar* (*Transcend and Organize*), Garzanti, Milan 1971, p. 18 (italics in original) (my translation).

20 See Pier Paolo Pasolini, 'Il Pci ai giovani! (Appunti in versi per una poesia in prosa seguiti da una "Apologia")' ('The Italian Communist Party to the Youth! (Notes in Verse for a Prose Poem Followed by an "Apology")'), in *Empirismo eretico* (*Heretical Empiricism*), Garzanti, Milan 2000, p. 151.

21 See Recalcati, *The Telemachus Complex*.

22 Pasolini, 'Il Pci ai giovani!' ('The Italian Communist Party to the Youth!'), p. 155 (my translation). (Translator's note: The 'Via delle Botteghe Oscure' on which Pasolini is urging the youth to converge refers to the historical location of the Italian Communist Party headquarters.)

23 See St Paul, First Letter to the Corinthians 13: 1–13.

24 Pier Paolo Pasolini, 'Le critiche del Papa' ('The Pope's Criticism'), in *Il caos* (*The Chaos*), Editori Riuniti, Rome 1981, p. 47 (italics in original) (my translation).